A KID'S GUIDE TO
AFRICAN AMERICAN HISTORY

MORE THAN 70 ACTIVITIES

NANCY I. SANDERS

CHICAGO
REVIEW
PRESS

To all my friends at Sisters in Christ Bible
Study. Your prayers, encouragement, and
support helped make this dream a reality.

To Rosa Parks.
Little did I know, when I saw you speak,
of the impact your life would have on me.

To Bessie Jones,
who inspired me as I read about her life.
May her memories and heritage live on
for generations to come.

Library of Congress Cataloging-in-Publication Data

Sanders, Nancy I.
  A Kid's guide to African American history / Nancy I. Sanders. — 2nd ed.
     p. cm.
  Includes bibliographical references and index.
  ISBN-13: 978-1-55652-653-4
  ISBN-10: 1-55652-653-9
  1. African Americans—History—Juvenile literature. 2. African Americans—
History—Study and teaching—Activity programs—Juvenile literature. I. Title.

E185.S19 2007
973'.0496073—dc22

2006031670

Cover and interior illustrations and design: Rattray Design

The author and the publisher disclaim all liability for use of the information
contained in this book.

The author has made every effort to secure permissions for all the material
quoted in this book. If any acknowledgment has inadvertently been omitted,
please contact the publisher.

Published by Chicago Review Press, Incorporated
814 North Franklin Street
Chicago, Illinois 60610
ISBN-13: 978-1-55652-653-4
ISBN-10: 1-55652-653-9
Printed in the United States of America
5 4 3 2

❧ Contents ❧

4 ❋ FREE AFRICAN AMERICANS AND ABOLITIONISTS

5 ❋ CIVIL WAR AND THE ROAD TO FREEDOM

6 ✸ THE TURN OF THE CENTURY

7 ✸ THE CIVIL RIGHTS MOVEMENT

8 ✸ HOPE FOR TODAY AND A BETTER TOMORROW

Time Line

The Glories of Africa

*3100 B.C.	Menes, the first pharaoh of united Egypt begins his reign
*1379 B.C.	Nefertiti, Queen of Egypt, begins her co-rule of Egypt
*A.D. 1500	Timbuktu, one of the greatest cities of the world is established
1527	Estavanico explores the American Southwest

Colonial America

1619	Twenty Africans land at Jamestown, Virginia
1641	Slavery is legally recognized in the colonies
1770	Crispus Attucks is the first to die in the American Revolution
1807	Congress bans ships from bringing slaves to America
1843	Sojourner Truth speaks out against slavery

Abolitionists

1849	Harriet Tubman escapes from slavery and begins work on the Underground Railroad

* Approximate date

Civil War

1861   Civil War begins

1863   President Lincoln signs the Emancipation Proclamation

1865   Thirteenth Amendment ends slavery in America

Freedom's Road

1881   Booker T. Washington establishes the Tuskegee Institute

1903   W. E. B. Du Bois publishes *The Souls of Black Folk*

1909   National Association for the Advancement of Colored People
(NAACP) is founded

1920s   The Harlem Renaissance, a time when extraordinary works are
created by musicians, artists, and writers, reaches its peak

1936   Jesse Owens wins four Olympic gold medals

Civil Rights Movement

1955   Rosa Parks is arrested

1961   Freedom Rides take place

1963   The March on Washington is held

A New Hope

1966   The first celebration of Kwanzaa is held

1967   Thurgood Marshall is appointed as a Supreme Court justice

1976   Black History Month is established

1986   National holiday is created to honor Dr. King

❋ Acknowledgments ❋

Thank you, Jeff, for your enthusiasm for this book. I appreciate the many times you alert me to current events in the news to help keep this information up-to-date. And thanks, Danny and Ben, for your continued enthusiasm and interest in my writing projects. You guys are the best!

Thank you, Evelyn Okoreeh, my dear, sweet friend. Your prayers and encouragement sustain me.

A special thank you goes to all the historians whose intense research and accurate facts help make it possible for me to share African American history with kids. Your books line my bookshelves and are friendly faces that greet me each day I sit down in my office to write. Among the many historians whose outstanding work I constantly refer to, I would especially like to express my appreciation to Carter Woodson, Charles W. Wesley, Benjamin Quarles, Lerone Bennett Jr., Darlene Clark Hine, Jessie Carney Smith, and Henry Louis Gates Jr.

Without the enthusiasm of certain individuals who have helped me gather important research, writing this edition would have been more difficult. I would especially like to thank Deborah Padgett from the Jamestown-Yorktown Foundation, Susan Halpert from the Houghton Library, and Sheila Cooke-Kayser, Emily G. Prigot, and Dr. Martin Blatt of the Boston National Historical Park.

Thanks to the entire publishing family at Chicago Review Press. It takes a team to bring a book to life, and you all are appreciated for the countless hours of creative energy you devoted to this project. Thank you, Cynthia Sherry, for your continued vision of this project. And thank you, Michelle Schoob, for stepping up to the editorial plate to help make this second edition a winner.

❊ Introduction ❊

You probably learned that Columbus explored America in 1492, but did you know that when Columbus landed in America, he heard stories of courageous blacks who had already arrived before him from across the ocean to trade gold with the Native Americans? You've learned how the Pilgrims landed at Plymouth Rock. But did you know that before the *Mayflower* ever set sail, there were already African Americans living in Jamestown, Virginia? And when you reach for the light switch, you might remember Thomas Edison, but did you know that Lewis H. Latimer, an African American, invented a way to make a lightbulb last even longer?

When people used to write history books, they often skipped over important things done by African Americans. But today, researchers show us that African Americans have made amazing discoveries and outstanding accomplishments. Through hard work, intelligence, faith, and determination, African Americans helped build the strong nation of America and are still impacting the world today.

The history of African Americans is a story that is both triumphant and sad. Through the many sufferings of slavery and discrimination emerged individuals and eventually a group of people who have made a difference in the lives of others.

Come along and join in the adventures you'll discover in this book. Participate in the historically based activities. Carve a miniature sandstone column similar to the one found in the ruins of a beautiful Ethiopian temple. Make a medallion just like the famous one that was used to persuade people to stop slavery. Tell a Brer Rabbit story echoing the ones told in the South. Design a brand similar to the ones black cowboys used on cattle in the

West. Learn about nonviolent protests, just like students during the Civil Rights Movement. Celebrate Kwanzaa and honor the history and pride of an extraordinary group of people. As you do all these things, and more, the story and the heritage of African Americans will come to life.

What's in a Name?

This book is the history of a group of people stolen away from their home and forced to work as slaves in an unknown land. Having lost everything, these people sought to restore their heritage, even through the identification of a specific name. Today they are proudly known as African Americans.

Here is a brief history of how the term *African American* came to be used.

* In 1619, when a group of indentured servants landed in Jamestown, Virginia, John Rolfe wrote in his diary, "A Dutch ship sold us 20 Negars."
* Slaves were often referred to as *Africans*, which identified them with their roots.
* During the 1800s, slave workers in a plantation house began calling themselves *colored* to show they were different from the workers in the field. Many had both black and white parents or grandparents.
* From the 1830s to the 1860s, many people didn't want to be called *African* anymore. Most of their families now lived in America.
* In 1890, Booker T. Washington encouraged the use of the word *Negro* to bring unity.
* In the 1960s, the term *black* gained respect through the Civil Rights Movement.
* Today, the term *African American* identifies this group of people with a homeland as well as the important history and culture they have developed in the United States.

Any titles or terms used in this book are not used to offend anyone, but as a reflection of the era being discussed.

1
The Glories of Africa

History is often silent about many things that happened long, long ago. Nobody is living today who can give us firsthand accounts of events many years before we were born. But we have clues that help us discover important things about the past. Special scientists called archaeologists (say it: ark-ee-ALL-uh-gists) use these clues to help us understand what Africa was like hundreds of years ago.

There are pictures on the tombs of Egyptian pharaohs (say it: FAIR-ohs) showing dark-skinned rulers as well as light-

skinned ones. Queen Nefertari (say it: nef-fer-TAR-ee), one of the most famous figures known today from Egypt, has been identified as black. There are ancient documents listing important victories and accomplishments by kings from African countries. Stories have been passed down from generation to generation describing the glories and wonders that used to exist. All these clues, and more, paint a picture to help us understand what ancient Africa was really like.

Prior to 800 B.C., the dark-skinned people from Ethiopia (say it: EE-thee-OH-pee-ah)

1

in Africa had important contact with ancient Egypt. They traded goods and materials back and forth. They fought wars with each other. They married each other and had children.

The fact that the color of their skin was different did not seem to matter very much to them.

For many years, Ethiopia had to pay taxes to Egypt and was under Egypt's rule. However, in the eighth century B.C., the Ethiopians went to war against the Egyptians and won. For more than a hundred years, the land was ruled by Ethiopian pharaohs.

Around 400 B.C., people in Africa made important progress and accomplished great achievements. In the years known as the African metal age, Africans worked with metals such as iron, copper, tin, silver, and bronze. They built large cities where crafters developed skills in leather, glass, gold, and weaving. They planted many crops. A huge system of trading developed. It was an age of progress and excitement.

Menes
(lived around 3100 B.C.)

Tradition says that the African king Menes (say it: mens) united Upper Egypt and Lower Egypt into one strong kingdom. With this union began the long line of pharaohs who ruled Egypt for 3,000 years. During the time of Menes, hieroglyphic writing developed. Technical skills, arts, and governmental institutions were improved during his rule.

A Sandstone Column

Some of the Ethiopian rulers were known for building beautiful temples and monuments. A sandstone column still stands, carved with many detailed designs, in the ruins of an Ethiopian temple. With this activity, you can make a replica.

Materials

Adult supervision required
1 cup (200 g) clean sand
½ cup (60 g) cornstarch
1 teaspoon (5 g) cream of
   tartar
Old cooking pot

Wooden spoon
¾ cup (177 ml) hot
   water
Paper drinking cup
Paper plate
Toothpicks

Dump the sand, cornstarch, and cream of tartar into the old pot. Use the wooden spoon to stir the mixture well. Add the hot water and cook over medium heat. Stir well until the mixture of sand is too thick to stir any more. Cool slightly and then spoon the mixture into a cup, tightly packing down the sand. Turn the cup upside down over a paper plate and let the sand mixture dump out to form a column on the plate. (You may need to squeeze the end of the paper cup to get it started.) Smooth the sides of the column with your hands. Use a tooth-pick to carve designs in your sandstone column like the one pictured here.

Design a Mask

African sculpture is known for its variety of styles, different designs, and great strength portrayed in the characters. Researchers have found African sculpture in many forms, including masks.

Materials

Illustrations of mask

Typing paper

Pencil

Scissors

1 9 by 11-inch (48 by 28 cm) sheet of black poster board

1 9 by 11-inch (48 by 28 cm) sheet of white poster board

Glue

White cotton household string

Use the illustration of the mask as a guide to trace the nose, eyes, and mouth onto typing paper. Cut these out and use them as a pattern to cut the pieces from black poster board. Cut the outline of the face out of white poster board. Glue the nose, eyes, and mouth to the face. Spread glue on the area of the white poster board that isn't covered by the nose, eyes, or mouth. Carefully glue short pieces of string in rows over the white poster board to resemble the original, carved design of the mask.

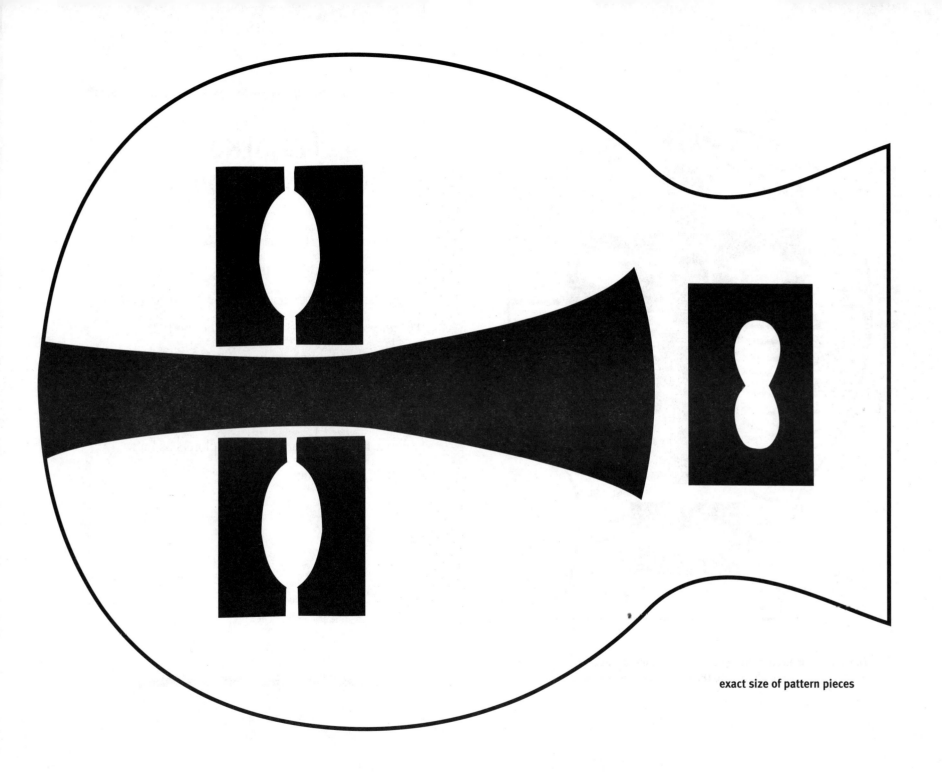

exact size of pattern pieces

The finished mask has the eyes, nose, and mouth made out of black poster board glued onto the white poster board head.

Taharka
(lived around 690 B.C.)

Taharka (say it: tah-HAR-kah) is known as the most important of the Ethiopian pharaohs. An outstanding leader, some people called him the "Emperor of the World." He ruled for about 25 years. During his reign, he brought many cultural improvements to his empire. He built many temples. He encouraged trade between Egypt and Ethiopia. He also led a group of explorers as far as the Strait of Gibraltar.

The Middle Ages

Africa was rich in gold. Traders arrived from the north with large groups, or caravans, of more than 12,000 camels at a time. The camels carried heavy loads of salt, sugar, wheat, fruit, and fabric across the dry Sahara Desert until they reached the kingdoms in West Africa of Ghana (say it: GAH-nah), Mali (say it: MAH-lee), and Songhay. Why did the traders travel so far and on such dangerous journeys across the hot desert? What did the traders want? They wanted the gold of Africa.

The kingdoms of Ghana, Mali, and Songhay grew powerful and wealthy by trading their gold and other products to the caravans from the north. By the Middle Ages, they had developed banking systems, school systems, and entire systems of law.

The kings of these kingdoms were unbelievably rich. One ruler of Ghana lived in a splendid castle filled with sculpture and decorated with beautiful windows. This ruler kept an army of 200,000 fighting men. Soldiers in the armies of these rulers often wore chain mail, a type of armor, and rode horses. Troops carried impressive shields and armed themselves with swords and lances.

The City of Timbuktu

By the 15th century, the kingdom of Songhay dominated the area with power. The city of Timbuktu (say it: tim-buck-TOO) in Songhay became an intellectual center where people traveled from far away to experience its dazzling excitement and study with its scholars.

During this time, Timbuktu was home to more than 100,000 people. The towers of two important mosques (say it: mosks) stood high above the other buildings. Flat-roofed buildings spread out across the city.

Moslem youths came to study law, math, and medicine at the University of Sankore in Timbuktu. Scholars came to Timbuktu to study its large collections of manuscripts, which included famous selections from Greek and Arabic literature. Scholars came to write their own books, too. The trading of books brought in more money than almost any other kind of business. The kings paid judges, doctors, and writers a large amount of money to do their jobs. People enjoyed dancing, fencing, gymnastics, and chess. Great respect was paid to learned people in this intellectual center of West Africa.

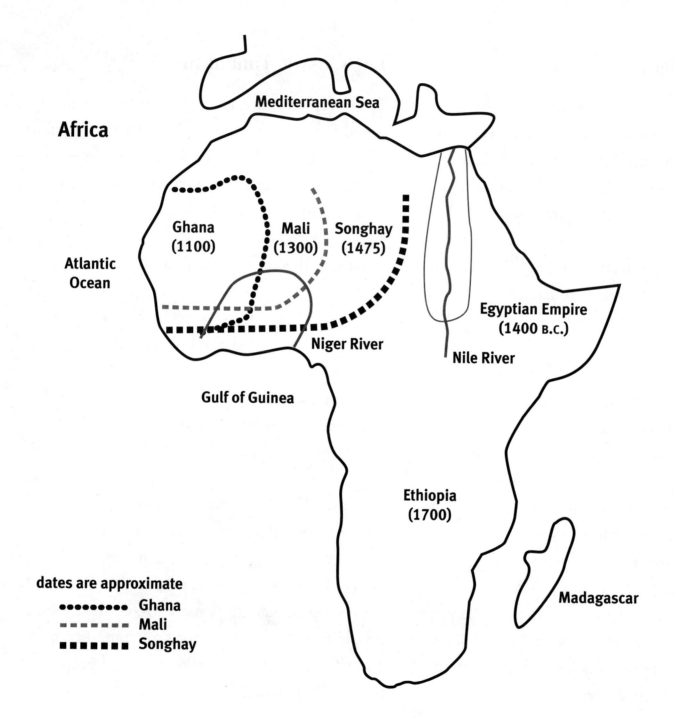

Africa

Mediterranean Sea

Ghana
(1100)

Mali
(1300)

Songhay
(1475)

Atlantic
Ocean

Egyptian Empire
(1400 B.C.)

Niger River

Nile River

Gulf of Guinea

Ethiopia
(1700)

Madagascar

dates are approximate

●●●●●●● Ghana

▬ ▬ ▬ ▬ ▬ Mali

■■■■■■■ Songhay

8

Potato Stamp Painting

Some artists painted Timbuktu during the Middle Ages to show a city made of square and round buildings. In the center of the pictures, they showed a tall mosque towering over the city. You can make a stamp from a potato to paint a picture of Timbuktu as it might have appeared during the Middle Ages.

Materials

Adult supervision required
1 potato, uncooked
Table knife, not sharp
Tempera paint
Shallow tray or bowl
Construction paper
Cotton swab

Use the table knife to cut a potato in half. One half of the potato will be used to stamp pictures of square houses. Cut away the flat side of the potato to form a raised square. Carve a small doorway in the square. The other half will be used to stamp pictures of round houses. Carve a small doorway on the flat part of this potato.

Spread a shallow amount of paint in the tray. Dip the potato halves in the paint, and paint a picture of Timbuktu by stamping round and square buildings in rows across the construction paper. In the center of the picture, paint a large building that represents one of the great mosques in the city. Use the cotton swab to paint the tall, thin tower at the top of the mosque. This is how some artists have painted Timbuktu during the Middle Ages.

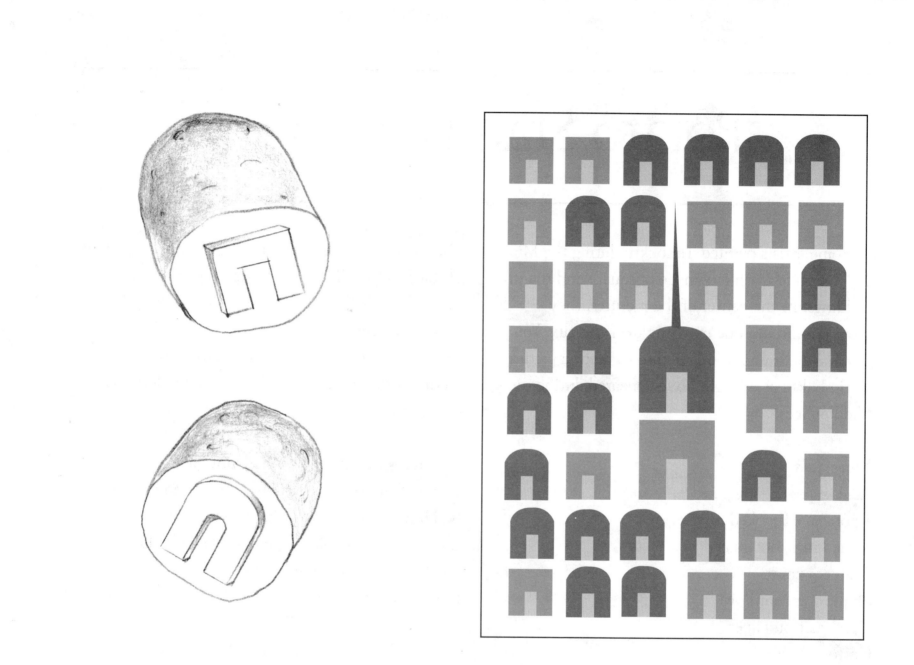

Potato halves

Picture of Timbuktu

A King's Scepter

In great cities such as Timbuktu, many people were well educated and enjoyed a wealthy lifestyle. Kings and rulers were among the wealthiest of all. They dressed in splendid clothes, wore beautiful jewelry, held fancy swords, and sometimes carried scepters made of gold.

Materials

Adult supervision required

Scissors

2 paper bowls (plastic or Styrofoam do not work as well)

2- or 3-foot (61 or 92-cm) long cardboard tube from gift wrapping paper

Glue

Styrofoam ball about 2 inches (5 cm) in diameter

Gold acrylic craft paint

Paintbrush

Use the scissors to carefully cut a hole in the bottom center of each bowl. The holes should measure the same size as the diameter of the cardboard tube. Slide the two bowls, rims facing each other, onto one end of the cardboard tube, about ¼-inch down from the edge. Use a small amount of glue to hold them in place. Glue the rims of the bowls together. Allow to dry.

Glue the Styrofoam ball onto the cardboard tube, just above the bowls. Paint the entire scepter gold.

Life in Africa

The Continent

Africa is a vast land with a variety of climates—jungles, deserts, rain forests, mountains, and lakes. The Nile River flows in the northeast. The Congo River crosses the equator twice. Grasslands are found in the west. Animals such as elephants, lions, and giraffes live there.

There were many wild and untamed areas in ancient Africa, but research has shown us that there were also many places of progress and culture. In the Nile Valley, archaeological discoveries tell us that Stone Age Africans made pottery and greatly influenced the success of ancient Egypt. Classical writers, such as Homer and Herodotus from Greece, tell of the glorious empires found in northern and central Africa. People traveled from far away to come to Africa's kingdoms, where elaborate networks of trade were built because of the abundance of gold, silver, and salt.

Family Life

The family was very important. Often, family lines of heritage were traced down through the mother, known as a matrilineal (say it: mat-rih-LIN-ih-al) line of descent. In many societies, a husband would leave his own home and join the family of his wife when they married. This was because in a matrilineal society, all the wealth, property, and possessions were passed on through the mother.

Family members who died were held in great honor because death was considered the beginning of a new life. Gifts were placed on graves to show respect and love for the ancestors.

Faith meant a lot to each individual. Religion was an important part of everyday life. Nature was treated with great respect. People took special care of natural resources such as water and trees.

Call-and-Response Game

Music was everywhere. Complicated and beautiful dances were developed. Two basic types of music could be found. One used a variety of drums and percussion instruments. The second type used a call-and-response pattern where the song leader called out and then a chorus of people responded, sounding like a chant.

Here is a children's game you can play with your friends. It's based on the call-and-response pattern, and it is still played in Africa today.

The song leader begins by asking, "What is big?" The other children respond in a chanting chorus saying, "Elephant is big." As the song continues, the song leader chooses other animals to ask about, listing large animals such as a giraffe or rhinoceros. (The song leader can repeat the names of animals during the song.) The children chant back their answer each time. However, if the song leader calls out the name of a small animal such as a bird or a mouse, children should not respond! Those who accidentally respond are out of the game. The song continues until there is only one player left in the game. This player becomes the new song leader.

What Is Big?

Leader: What is big?
Chorus: Elephant is big.
Leader: What is big?
Chorus: Elephant is big
         Among all the animals of the world.
         There is none larger.

Continue playing the game in this manner. Be sure not to say anything if the suggested animal isn't actually big, or you'll be out of the game.

Here are examples of other verses you can create.

Leader: Giraffe is big?
Chorus: Giraffe is big.
Leader: Giraffe is big?
Chorus: Giraffe is big.
          Among all the animals of the world
          There is none larger.
Leader: Bird is big?
(Silence)

Reprinted with permission of Simon & Schuster from *Juba This and Juba That: 100 African-American Games for Children* by Dr. Darlene Powell Hopson and Dr. Derek S. Hopson with Thomas Clavin.

Copyright ©1996 by Darlene Powell Hopson, Derek Hopson, and Thomas Clavin.

Communities and Nations

Many communities in Africa were agrarian. Different farming skills and techniques developed depending on which part of Africa a group lived in, or the climate and land formations present. Some communities in areas along the midwestern coastline knew how to cultivate rice, and others specialized in growing corn, cotton, or other crops. An important trade system developed between these communities and other areas of the world.

Some nations grew very advanced in their weaving skills. Other nations developed better ways of working with metal. Most nations, however, had a system of money that was based on the use of cowrie shells, a small seashell. (Say it: COW-ree.) Before the Europeans arrived and built up the slave trade that changed the way of life for thousands of people, life in Africa was based on family heritage, cultural developments, and national pride.

2
Colonial America

In 1492, Christopher Columbus set sail across the Atlantic Ocean and discovered what became known as the "New World." Today, we understand that many different native peoples were already living on the continents of North and South America, but to the citizens living in countries such as Spain, France, and Portugal, this "New World" was a place to be explored and conquered in the name of their kings or queens. The race to colonize the Americas began.

For about 100 years, Spain dominated the attempts to colonize, or settle, North and South America. Gold was discovered, silver mines were dug, and cities were conquered. Black and white conquistadors (say it: con-KEY-sta-doors), Spanish soldiers, fought side by side, even though most soldiers of African descent were enslaved. It was a dangerous time, and few names were recorded on expeditions where even well-known heroes such as Columbus or Balboa could be arrested or put in chains if they didn't find enough gold and other riches to satisfy the king or queen. Some names were written down, however. We know of heroic men such as Juan Valiente, black conquistador of Chile, and Juan Garcia and Miguel Ruiz, black conquistadors of Peru. Sometimes the king of Spain rewarded their service with a salary or allotment of land.

Soon other sailors, explorers, settlers, and slaves arrived by the boatload from various ports along the coast of Europe and Africa. In the 1550s, Portugal began building huge plantations of sugarcane in Brazil to satisfy the sweet tooth of wealthy Europeans. By the mid-1600s, France established colonies in places such as Haiti. England joined in the race and sent boatloads of men, women, and children to settle in colonies along the shores of North America.

Early Explorers

Since the earliest explorers arrived on the shores of the New World, blacks have had an important part in the exploration and development of North and South America. Archaeological finds from early Mexico of carved African images, as well as signs of African customs and ceremonies, suggest that fleets of Africans traveled across the Atlantic Ocean to trade and explore as early as 1400 B.C.

Gigantic stone heads, each weighing up to 40 tons and some standing nine feet tall have been found in an area of Central America where a group of people known as the Olmecs once lived. The faces on these statues, dating from around 800 B.C., appear to be African. Graveyards have also been found nearby with skeletons which are thought to be of people from Africa long, long ago.

The famous king of Mali, Abubakari (say it: uh-byoo-buh-CAR-ee; also known as Mansa Musa II) ruled over his wealthy African kingdom in the early 1300s. He organized two fantastic voyages to explore the Atlantic Ocean and beyond. According to tradition, the king himself led the second expedition where more than 2,000 ships sailed across the sea. He was never heard from again in his own country. But when Columbus, Balboa, and other European explorers arrived in the Americas nearly 200 years later, their journals, letters, and records show that they found small pockets of African communities, suggesting that Abubakari's expeditions were a success.

When Christopher Columbus sailed across the ocean in 1492, it's believed that at least one of the men aboard ship was of African heritage. His name was Pedro Alonzo Niño. His work was to pilot and help navigate, or keep the ship on course.

Three hundred Africans were with Hernando Cortés when the famed Aztecs of Mexico were defeated. Black conquistador, freeman, and explorer Juan Garrido served the Spanish Crown for 30 years in its conquest of Mexico and the Aztec empire. Garrido fought with Cortés to take over what is now known as Mexico City. After one key battle, Garrido built a small chapel to honor the soldiers from Spain who had died in the fight. He is also famous for being the first person to plant and harvest wheat in the Americas. Garrido planted seeds brought over from Spain.

Nuflo de Olano, an enslaved conquistador and explorer, joined the men on Balboa's daring expedition that hacked its way through steaming jungle to cross the Isthmus of Panama. Along with 30 Africans, 190 Spaniards, and 1,000 Native Americans, de Olano was with Balboa in 1513 when they first saw the Pacific Ocean.

Africans were with Pizarro in Peru and Ponce de Leon in Florida. Many other explorers also had Africans in their expeditions as officers, sailors, freemen, servants, and slaves. These daring men came to the New World and explored its vast, unknown lands.

Estevanico (?-1539)

Remembered for his bravery and ability as an explorer, Estevanico (say it: es-tay-vah-NEE-ko) traveled with Spanish expeditions to explore the New World. He was an advisor to Cortés as well as a guide to Cabeza de Vaca. Estevanico explored land including Florida, Arizona, and New Mexico. His last and most famous expedition took him in search of the famous "Seven Cities of Gold," where he scouted ahead of the rest of his party, accompanied by two large greyhounds and several Native American guides. Estevanico thought he found what he was searching for when he came upon the Seven Cities of the Zuni Indians in New Mexico. However, he was killed when he tried to enter the cities. A couple of his guides returned to his friends to tell of his discovery and his death.

First Settlers

Many attempts were made to establish settlements in what is now known as the United States. Most of the time, these settlements failed because of dangerous battles with Native Americans, fatal diseases, or the difficulties of trying to survive in untamed wilderness. Spain tried to build a colony in South Carolina in 1526. A group of enslaved Africans was with this group. Unable to survive the harsh wilderness and afraid of attack from the natives, the Spaniards left, leaving the Africans behind. Many of them survived, becoming part of the Native American communities in that region.

Spanish explorers also attempted to establish a settlement in the mid-1500s along the shore of the Gulf of Mexico in the region where Alabama is today. When the settlement failed, at least one African remained behind to settle in with the Native Americans.

Both free and enslaved African explorers were members of the Spanish expedition to establish the oldest successful settlement of Europeans in the

United States. St. Augustine, Florida, was founded in 1565. Africans were influential in the success of this settlement. These men were experts in blacksmithing, woodworking, and military defense. Their knowledge of farming and cattle raising helped guarantee a steady food supply for the new colonists.

Landing in Jamestown

In 1619, one year before the *Mayflower* set sail with the Pilgrims for America, a ship named the *White Lion* landed in Jamestown, Virginia. On the ship were about 20 Africans. According to records, these Africans were sold as indentured servants to help John Rolfe and the other English colonists harvest tobacco and survive among the wilderness conditions they found in the New World.

Originally from the kingdom of Ndongo (say it: en-DON-go) in Angola, Africa, they were excellent farmers. They knew how to grow yams, grains, corn, and tobacco. They were also skilled ironworkers. As blacksmiths, they knew how to make tools such as iron hoes and weapons such as iron axe

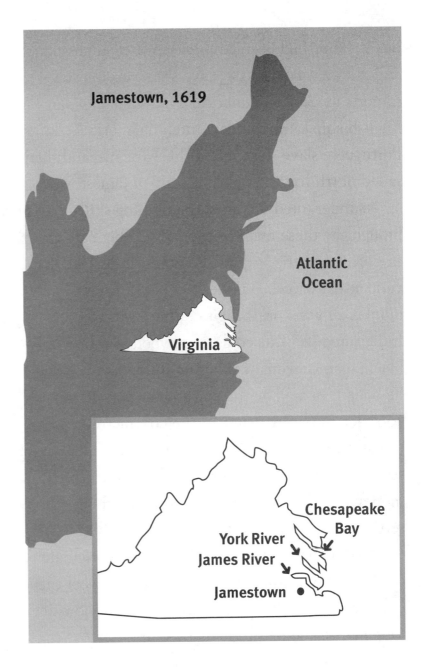

heads. They had been captured in their homeland and put on a Portuguese slave ship carrying slaves to ports in Central America. The *White Lion*, an English ship sailing under Dutch flags, attacked the Portuguese slave ship, seized the Africans, and then sailed north to the English colony of Jamestown.

As indentured servants, the farming skills brought by these first Africans were a big part of the success of the Virginia colonies. Indentured servants usually worked under a contract for a certain number of years until their contract was paid up. Indentured servants could be anybody—white or black, man or woman, adult or child. They could be bought or sold by the person who owned the contract. When the time of the contract was up, usually after a period of seven years, the indentured servants were freed. Sometimes they were given money, clothes, or small plots of land to help them settle in the community.

By 1651, several of the Africans who originally landed in Jamestown had fulfilled the terms of their contracts as indentured servants and were now free. One man named Antony married another African named Isabella, who had also arrived in Jamestown on the ship in 1619. They had a baby and named him William. William was the first black born in the English colonies in America whose birth was officially recorded.

There was a short period of time, about 40 years, when African Americans were treated with a measure of equality and lived their lives much as other colonists did. Anthony Johnson, another African who was probably an indentured servant at this time, eventually earned his freedom. He married a woman named Mary and together they had four children. Anthony and Mary owned land, buying indentured servants of their own. The family later settled in Maryland. In 1666, Anthony signed a lease to rent a plot of land. This lease can still be found among historical records today.

African Americans also voted during this short time and held political office, just like the other pioneers did in the New World. African Americans could obtain their freedom from indentured servitude and establish themselves as part of the American colonies.

The Beginning of Slavery

Life was hard in the New World. Fields needed to be cleared by chopping down trees and digging up stumps. Crops had to be planted and cared for as they grew, in order to have enough food to eat and clothes to wear. Forts and houses often burned down from fires and needed to be rebuilt. It was hard work for anyone to do, but especially for wealthy businessmen from England who were only used to office work, or no work at all!

As colonies were first started in America, indentured servants arrived by the boatload to do most of the back-breaking work that needed to be done. Orphaned children, prisoners, and other people living in poverty in overcrowded, unhealthy jails, or in other terrible conditions in England and other European countries signed on as indentured servants, or were forced to do so. They came across the ocean to work and be sold to the person who paid the highest price for their contract.

However, workers couldn't arrive fast enough to meet the growing demand. The colonists tried capturing Native Americans and enslaving them, but they soon realized this didn't work very well. Native Americans would escape and disappear into the forests or return to their homes, never to be found again. Also, many Native Americans quickly died from measles, smallpox, and other diseases the Europeans brought to the New World.

The demand for workers grew. John Rolfe and others discovered that conditions in the New World were perfect for growing tobacco, and there was a high demand for tobacco in Europe, where it brought high prices. Tobacco thus became an important crop in the colonies. It took many workers to plant and harvest tobacco, many more workers than the number of indentured servants who arrived each year on boats.

Colonial farmers also grew other crops, such as rice, cotton, and indigo, a plant which could make a beautiful blue dye used in clothing. A huge number of workers were needed to raise these crops, in order to meet the demand for these goods and make it profitable to ship them to England.

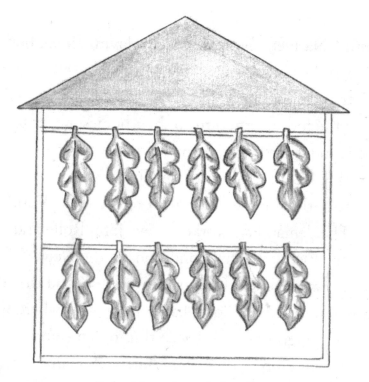

Drying tobacco leaves by hanging.

The slave trade was already in operation in various parts of the world. Colonists heard how slavery provided enough workers in South America and in the Caribbean to grow sugar on the enormous sugar plantations there. American colonists began buying slaves brought over from Africa to do the hard work necessary to grow and harvest their crops.

An African slave could be bought for life during the late 1600s for about $150. This is the same amount it would cost to buy an English indentured servant for seven years! If they tried to escape as the Native Americans had, African slaves couldn't return home easily because their homes were on the other side of the Atlantic Ocean. If African slaves did escape, they were easy to find because their dark skin was different from that of the English colonists. Also, there were no laws to protect Africans in the New World, while an indentured servant who was overworked or mistreated could appeal to the courts of England. For these reasons and others, more colonists began purchasing slaves.

While the colonists in America were busy making laws about equality and freedom for themselves, new laws were also being written about slavery. States wrote laws called slave codes that said slaves were not allowed to do things such as learn to read or write. The slave codes even said that it was against the law for slaves to get married. One by one, these new laws took away all the personal rights of Africans who were brought to America and forced to live as slaves in a new and unfamiliar land.

Fort Mose

While the British were busy establishing colonies along the eastern shore of present-day America, Spain's settlement at St. Augustine, Florida, continued to flourish. In 1670, the English colony of Charles Town was established in South Carolina. Within 10 years, enslaved African Americans from English settlements in Charles Town and other communities in South Carolina and Georgia began making a series of daring escapes. These fugitives headed south to Spanish-controlled territory. At St. Augustine, runaway slaves from the English colonies were offered freedom if they agreed to convert to Catholicism and serve the Spanish Crown. They served the king in a variety of positions, receiving salaries as paid employees. Some worked as cooks in the governor's house. Others worked as blacksmiths to make weapons and tools. Still others helped build the Castillo de San Marcos.

The Castillo de San Marcos is the oldest masonry fort in America. Free blacks worked side by side with Native Americans and Spaniards to build this strong defense to protect the colony of St. Augustine.

In 1693, King Charles II of Spain wrote an official proclamation giving legal sanction to fugitive slaves arriving in Spanish territory. The news spread like wildfire.

An early kind of Underground Railroad formed. Free blacks, Native Americans, and Spanish settlers helped slaves escape on a dangerous route south from English colonies to St. Augustine. This was more than a century before the Underground Railroad would help slaves escape north in the years leading up to the Civil War. Men, women, and children escaped by walking, on horseback, or by boat.

Francisco Menendez, originally from Africa, escaped slavery and fled to St. Augustine. As a freeman, he joined the militia and rose up through the ranks to become captain. In 1738, Menendez was put in charge of the community of Gracia Real de Santa Teresa de Mose (Fort Mose) just two miles north of St. Augustine. Fort Mose (say it: moh-SAY) was a community of free blacks, the first of its kind in the history of the United States. About 100 fugitive slaves settled in this fortified town.

Fort Mose was in a key geographical position. Just south of the British colonies, it was established as the northern outpost of Spanish-owned territory. It was the first line of defense against British troops marching south into Florida or launching attacks by sea. Over the years, Fort Mose's Black Militia put up a courageous and strong defense against various attacks until the Treaty of Paris in 1763. At this time, Florida was given to the British. Most of the free blacks from Fort Mose moved and resettled in Cuba.

The Slave Trade

When different nations in Africa went to war against each other, prisoners were often taken.

These prisoners were kept as captives. Sometimes the prisoners were exchanged for their own people who had been captured by their enemies. Sometimes the prisoners were given back as a way to stop the fighting. Sometimes the prisoners were kept as slaves.

Usually, these slaves in Africa were only made to work as hard as the other members of the community. They often married, and could rise to hold prominent positions in the village if they chose.

Europeans who traded goods with the nations of Africa noticed this practice of making prisoners of captive people from a warring community. Realizing that this might help solve the shortage of workers in the New World, these Europeans began trading goods in exchange for these African prisoners.

Once this type of trade began, it caught on like wildfire. European countries raced against each other to try to get the most money from this new trade of shipping African slaves to the New World. It might cost up to $13,000 to equip a ship, but the slaves who filled up the ship could then be sold for $220,000 when the ship arrived in America.

The slave trade to the New World lasted for several hundred years. Europeans brought to Africa weapons and guns that were much more powerful than the weapons already there. They traded these weapons for the prisoners of war who were already being held as captives. They also used powerful guns to attack entire villages, as they tried to capture as many Africans as they could.

Africans fought back fiercely to protect their villages, killing many Europeans. When the Europeans found how dangerous this was, they tried a different way to get more slaves. They started promising beads, fabric, liquor, and guns to any African who would bring them more slaves. They realized Africa was made up of many different nations and tribes that had their own languages and customs. Therefore, the traders encouraged Africans to take captives from their enemies' villages and bring the captives to their ships in exchange for these goods.

European and American trading companies formed in such cities as New York and London to organize the slave trade. The traders built forts along the western coast of Africa, called trading stations, which could hold enough Africans to fill a ship. Once the forts were built, people from the trading companies visited the different communities and promised the villagers weapons or other goods in exchange for prisoners. Out of fear for the safety of their own village, and needing guns to protect themselves from the slave traders, many Africans joined in the slave trade, capturing and selling people from other tribes.

Often, the captured Africans were forced to march many miles to the forts by the ocean where the slave ship waited, anchored out at sea. Slaves were marched to the fort, tied with chains or yoked together with forked branches. The leaders of the march were then given their payment in exchange for bringing the slaves.

Bead Necklace

Even though a bead necklace might not seem very important today, to a poor African, it could be worn as a symbol of importance or wealth. Africans who were involved in the slave trade were willing to turn their prisoners over to the traders in exchange for bead necklaces, weapons, and liquor.

Materials

Adult help suggested

Oven-bake clay (found in craft
   stores)

Toothpick

Sturdy wire that won't bend (such as
   hanger wire)

Quart-sized baking dish

Floss

Preheat the oven to 275°. To make the beads, make small round balls by rolling the clay in your hands. Use the toothpick to poke a hole through the center of each bead. String the beads on the wire and space them apart from each other. Place the wire across the baking dish so the beads won't flatten while they bake.

Bake the beads for 10 minutes. When the clay and the wire are cool, remove the beads from the wire. String them on a piece of floss that will fit over your head. Tie the ends of the floss together with a sturdy knot.

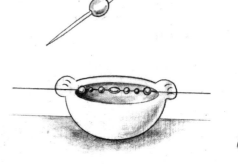

Abd al-Rahman Ibrahima (1762-1829)

Born in Africa, Abd al-Rahman Ibrahima was the son of a chief. At 12, Ibrahima was sent to Timbuktu for his education and Moslem training. In this great city, he learned to read and write Arabic and recite from the Koran. Upon completing his education, he returned home and continued his training to become a chief. Ibrahima got married and had several children.

One day, when he was about 25 years old, Ibrahima led a group of horsemen from his village in a battle against neighboring enemies. He was suddenly captured! Made to march many miles to the sea, he was sold and put on a slave ship heading to America. He survived the trip and landed in Mississippi to be sold as a slave. For more than 20 years he was forced to be a slave. He married again, but never stopped longing for his freedom. Finally, he wrote a letter asking for his freedom. His letter was originally sent to people in his native village, but by mistake it ended up in the hands of important Moroccan officials. These officials asked the American government to free Ibrahima. After many more letters, and help from abolitionists, Americans who were against slavery, Ibrahima and his wife were freed. They set sail to return to Africa, but Ibrahima died on the way back to his homeland.

The Middle Passage

Captured Africans were loaded onto slave ships that crossed the Atlantic Ocean. This trip was called the Middle Passage because it was the middle of the trip for a slave ship. First, the ship usually came from its homeland to Africa, carrying rum to trade for the captives. Next, the ship would take slaves across the Atlantic Ocean to North or South

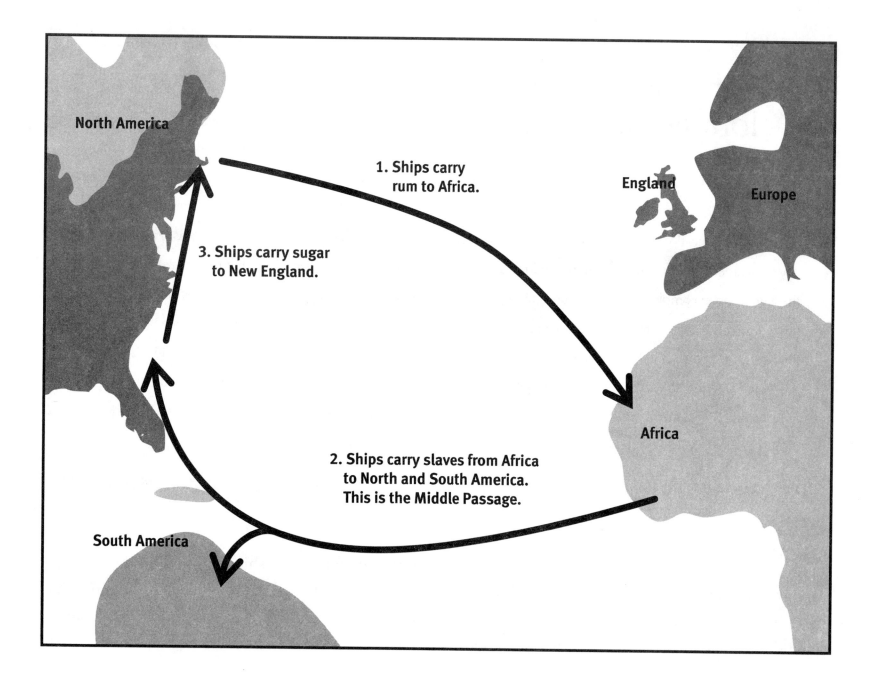

1. Ships carry rum to Africa.

2. Ships carry slaves from Africa to North and South America. This is the Middle Passage.

3. Ships carry sugar to New England.

North America

South America

England

Europe

Africa

America. Then, the ship would sail back to its homeland, often carrying sugar to be made into more rum.

Each ship usually had a captain and a crew of 8 to 15 men. The cargo hold on the ship was filled with slaves. Most ships tried to carry as many captured slaves as possible so they could sell them and get the most money. They did this even though it made the ship unsafe. Slaves were chained together and crowded so closely against each other that they couldn't move. Conditions were unbearable.

There were separate areas for the men, women, and children. Often, during the trip, there was a shortage of food and water. Diseases such as smallpox and other fevers swept through the ship, killing many of the people on board.

Landing in America

Slave ships often landed first in the West Indies. These islands are south of Florida. There were many large plantations in the West Indies that grew crops such as sugar and indigo. They also bought a lot of slaves. When the slave ships later landed in North America, the slaves were taken to be sold at the slave markets, which often took place at the county courthouse.

Whether Africans had been princes or chiefs, married or with children, at the slave market they were treated like cattle and sold without any care for their personal identity or feelings. They were simply lined up, looked at, and sold to the person who wanted to purchase them for the most money. A father, mother, and child could each be sold to different plantations and might never see each other again.

A ship's captain purchased each captive in Africa for about $25, or traded that much for each person in rum, fabric, beads, and weapons. Slaves were then sold in the slave markets in North American colonies for about $150 each.

The Revolutionary War

England ruled the colonies in North America. But when the king sent British soldiers over to make

Crispus Attucks
(1723?-1770)

Crispus Attucks was born into slavery. When he was 27, he ran away, joined the crew of a whaling ship, and taught himself to read and write. He later lived in Boston during a time of unrest. The king of England taxed the colonists and sent Redcoats, or British soldiers, to Boston to make sure the colonists paid their taxes. On March 5, 1770, Attucks led other colonists as they met a group of Redcoats. The two groups argued. A shot was fired, and Attucks was killed. Several other colonists were also killed. This became known as the Boston Massacre, the first of many events that led to the Revolutionary War.

sure the colonists obeyed the king's laws, the colonists began to talk of freedom and independence from England. Some slaves and free African Americans thought this talk might lead to their own freedom and independence. Therefore, many African Americans joined in the call for freedom. In the Boston Massacre (say it: MASS-ah-cur) of 1770, Crispus Attucks, along with an angry crowd protesting against unfair British laws, confronted a group of British soldiers. Attucks was shot along with several others, and was the first person to die for the cause of independence for America.

The Shot Heard Around the World

The colonists gathered an army together to stand against the British soldiers. These soldiers were called *minutemen* because they needed to be ready at a minute's notice.

African Americans signed up to be minutemen. Many were hoping the cry for freedom that was echoing throughout the land would also bring freedom to the slaves. Lemuel Haynes enlisted as a minuteman in Granville, Massachusetts. Peter Salem, a slave, was given his freedom so he could enlist as a minuteman in the militia from Framingham, Massachusetts. Prince Estabrooks, from Lexington, signed up with the minutemen in Captain John Parker's company.

As minutemen, these men, along with other African Americans, drilled side by side with white patriots on the village greens of their towns and communities. They learned to march, carry their guns, and take a united stand against British Redcoats.

In the early hours of April 19, 1775, Paul Revere rode on his famous ride through the countryside just outside of Boston. He called the minutemen to gather because British soldiers were marching to the town of Concord in hopes of capturing American guns that were secretly stored there. On that night, Prince Estabrooks, along with several other African Americans, reacted to Revere's cry, "The Regulars are out! The Regulars are out!" Prince Estabrooks and the others grabbed their guns and hurried to Lexington, the town closer to Boston.

Captain Parker's minutemen gathered on Lexington Green to face the marching Redcoats. When the first shot of the Revolutionary War was fired that morning, Prince Estabrooks took part in fighting for America's independence. After this first skirmish, he hurried down the road with his company to meet Peter Salem and other minutemen at Concord Bridge. By the time the British soldiers arrived, they were ready. Other shots rang out, and Prince Estabrooks was wounded.

The British headed back to Boston after the battle at Concord Bridge, burning houses and towns along the way. By this time, minutemen from communities around the countryside ran to join the fight. These minutemen hid behind rocks and fences all along the road, shooting the British soldiers on their retreat. By nightfall, the surviving Redcoats made it back to Boston and the protection of the cannon on the British warships floating in the harbor. The minutemen camped nearby, a safe distance away from the cannon. The Siege (say it: seej) of Boston began.

All throughout the area, minutemen were called to come join the siege. A siege is when an army surrounds a city for many days, not letting anyone in or out of the city. In the Siege of Boston, minutemen stationed themselves throughout the countryside all around Boston, refusing to let any Redcoats escape. Lemuel Haynes marched with the militia from Granville down to Roxbury, where they camped just outside of Boston.

Several weeks after the siege began, African American patriots such as Primas Black and Epheram Blackman joined the ranks of Ethan Allen and his Green Mountain Boys. As members of this band of soldiers, they were known for helping capture an important British fort called Fort Ticonderoga (say it: tie-con-der-OH-gah). The news of this important military victory cheered the militia who were keeping the British under siege at Boston.

Merchant Ships

The harbor at Philadelphia was a busy one, with many ships sailing in and out of port. However, there were only 31 ships in the Continental, or American, navy. To build their defense at sea against the powerful British navy, owners of smaller merchant ships were paid to have their ships outfitted with guns to fight in the war. James Forten, a free African American living in Philadelphia, sailed on one of these merchant ships during the Revolutionary War.

Materials

Brown and black construction paper, one sheet each

Pencil

Scissors

11 by 18-inch (28 by 46-cm) light blue construction paper

Glue

Heavy black thread, the kind used to sew on buttons

Several small triangles of colorful fabric

White facial tissues

Crayons

Epsom salts

Water

Cup or bowl

Paintbrush

To construct a 3-D picture of a sailing ship, first cut the shape of the bottom of the sailing boat from brown construction paper and glue it on the blue background construction paper. Cut thin strips of black construction paper for masts, the tall posts that hold the sails. Glue these masts on the ship, using the illustrations as a guide. Glue heavy black thread to represent the ropes for the sails. Add a fabric flag at the top of the center mast.

Cut tissue into squares or triangles to represent the sails. Glue on the sails, flat or appearing puffed out by the wind, by putting a spot of glue on each corner of the tissue, or roll up the sails and glue them on. After your ship is built, use blue or green crayons and lightly color the ocean.

Prepare a mixture of Epsom salts to make the ocean water. Mix ¼ cup (236 ml) Epsom salts with ¼ cup (236 ml) of warm water in a cup or bowl until the crystals dissolve. Use the paintbrush to paint the solution over the ocean in your picture. In a day or two, crystals will form, making the ocean look real.

James Forten
(1766-1842)

Best known as a founder of the Abolitionist (say it: ab-o-LIH-shin-ist) Movement (see chapter 4, page 103 for more information), African American James Forten was also a sailor, inventor, and wealthy businessman. At 15, he sailed against British ships during the Revolutionary War. After the war, he returned home to learn sail making, eventually buying the shop where he was trained. He invented a device that handled sails easier, and soon became wealthy. He purchased freedom for slaves, helped launch William Lloyd Garrison's newspaper *The Liberator*, and used his home as an Underground Railroad station (see page 127 for more information).

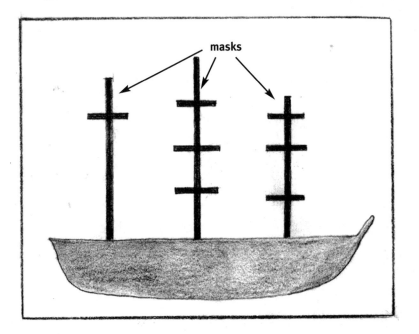

masks

heavy black thread

This is a ship with folded sails.

This ship is ready to sail.

Lemuel Haynes
(1753-1833)

Never knowing his black father and abandoned by his white mother, Lemuel Haynes was brought up as an indentured servant by a white family in Granville, Massachusetts. Receiving little formal education, he studied on his own hours. Deeply religious, he memorized entire passages of scriptures and frequently was called upon in his family circle to speak about God and the Bible. Passionate about the ideals of liberty and equality of all men, Haynes enlisted as a minuteman. He joined the Siege of Boston with his militia company and later served with the campaign to overtake Fort Ticonderoga and transport its cannon to the battlefront for use by the Continental Army. During the war, Haynes wrote a patriotic ballad about the Battle of Lexington. He also wrote a manuscript called "Liberty Further Extended: Or Free thoughts on the illegality of Slave-keeping." In this, Haynes expressed his strong views against slavery. After the American Revolution, Haynes continued his religious studies and became an important and well-known minister in New England.

The Battle of Bunker Hill

African Americans fought with courage in the Revolutionary War. They won awards and praise, and some were even given their freedom because of their bravery. They marched over land in the army and battled at sea in the navy. Some served as spies, risking their lives to sneak into British camps in search of important information.

During the Siege of Boston, Salem Poor camped out with his company of minutemen around the British troops holed up in Boston. When spies spread the news that the Redcoats planned to move out of Boston and overtake the nearby vantage point of Charlestown, Salem Poor and the other patriots took action. On the night of June 16, 1775, Salem Poor and his fellow soldiers snuck into Charlestown and went to work. When the sun rose early in the morning, the British were shocked to see fortifications and strong dirt embankments built up in the exact spot they had planned to overtake. The Redcoats charged, but were forced back. They charged again, but again the fighting was too fierce. They charged one last time, but by then most of

Wentworth Cheswill
(1748-1817)

During the American Revolution, the town of Newmarket, New Hampshire, voted to appoint Wentworth Cheswill to carry urgent messages by horseback to a network of patriots. His task was similar to Paul Revere's. A well-educated man at a time when few received formal education, Cheswill was committed to the patriot cause. He signed his name to a list willing to fight against the British. Volunteering as a private under Captain John Langdon, he marched with his company 250 miles to join the Continental Army in Saratoga. Active throughout the war, he returned to his home in Newmarket where he became a successful and prosperous businessman. Always interested in politics, Cheswill held a variety of positions including selectman, auditor, assessor, and scrivener. Cheswill's grandfather was a slave.

the minutemen had run out of ammunition. With heavy losses to both sides, the Redcoats used their bayonets to push patriot troops out of the newly built fort.

We don't know the exact details of what happened that day at the Battle of Bunker Hill. However, a petition filed a few months later gives us a clue about the courageous part Salem Poor took in the battle. Fourteen officers signed the petition stating that Salem Poor's heroic actions were like that of an "experienced officer, as well as an excellent soldier" and that Poor was a "brave and gallant soldier." Salem Poor continued to serve throughout the Revolutionary War, including at Saratoga, Valley Forge, and Monmouth.

Another hero of the Battle of Bunker Hill was Peter Salem. Having already seen action at Concord on the first day of fighting, Salem was known as an excellent shot. He is credited with shooting British Major Pitcairn during the battle.

Black Patriots in the American Revolution

At times, different groups tried to stop African Americans from joining the war. American slaveholders insisted that George Washington stop letting African Americans sign up as soldiers. But when the British promised freedom to any slave who joined the side of the king, Washington's army decided to include African American soldiers rather than having them fight for the enemy. Even though they weren't guaranteed their freedom, by joining Washington's army African Americans hoped that helping their government become free from British rule would help establish freedom for all races in America.

Colonel George Middleton organized a company in Boston called the Bucks of America. Military records don't show the exact service these troops gave to their country, but John Hancock was so impressed with their patriotism and courage that he presented a flag to Middleton as a tribute of his respect. This silk flag has the picture of a buck, or

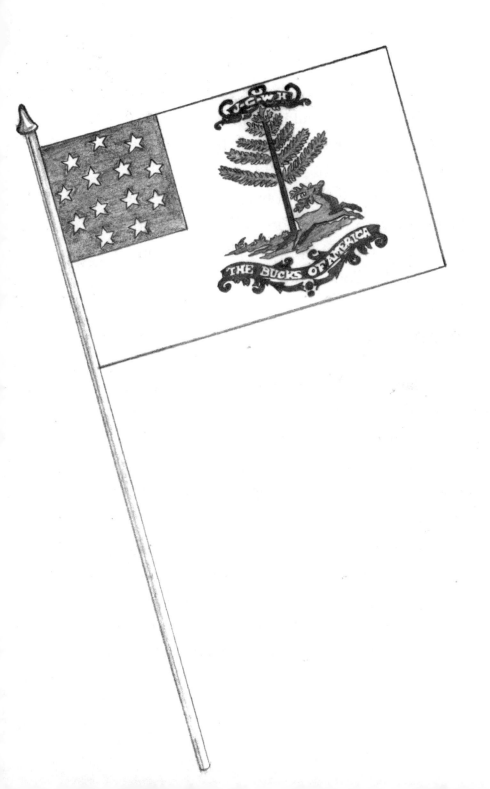

deer, standing underneath a pine tree, similar to the metal badge worn by the soldiers in this all-black unit.

When Rhode Island offered freedom to any slave who enlisted, the First Rhode Island Regiment was formed. Shortly after their initial training, they joined several white troops at the Battle of Rhode Island. This regiment of more than 90 ex-slaves and 30 freemen distinguished themselves by holding firm against three fierce attacks from British and Hessian (German) soldiers. As they bravely held their ground, their heroic fighting helped the American army escape safely behind them with all their equipment. The First Rhode Island Regiment continued to fight until the end of the war.

African Americans served during the war in a variety of capacities. Not only a soldier, Barzillai Lew was also a fifer (flute player) and drummer. He fought at the Battle of Bunker Hill as well as at other battles.

A young Richard Allen drove wagonloads of salt from the shores of the Atlantic Ocean to the troops inland. During the war, salt was more precious than gold to starving soldiers who needed salt to preserve meat for food. A dangerous job, salt drivers were often attacked by Redcoats or loyalists who supported the British.

Prince Whipple is best remembered as one of the oarsmen in Leutze's painting *Washington Crossing the Delaware*. Prince Whipple was a bodyguard to General Whipple, an aide to George Washington. As a youth, Prince Whipple's wealthy parents in Africa sent him to America to receive a formal education. Kidnapped by the boat's captain, Prince was sold as a slave to William Whipple some years before the American Revolution began.

One of the most important patriot spies was James Armistead Lafayette. Because of his bravery, loyalty, and espionage (say it: ES-pee-oh-nazh) skill, James was influential in finally bringing the Revolutionary War to an end. A slave from Virginia, James volunteered to serve under the French officer Marquis de Lafayette. During the siege at Yorktown, James carried important information back and forth between the British and patriot camps. Having convinced the British General Cornwallis that he would spy on the Americans, James actually spied on the British and secretly carried their battle plans to Lafayette. His skills as a double agent provided Washington's troops with the information they needed to force the British to surrender at Yorktown and thus bring a stunning victory to the Continental Army.

The War at Sea

At 15, James Forten was in the middle of the Revolutionary War. He saw the soldiers, black and white, marching through the streets of Philadelphia. He listened to the sailors, who docked their ships nearby and told exciting stories of great battles against England's ships.

Forten wanted to fight for the independence of his country. He signed up to join the crew on a ship called the *Royal Louis*. This ship and its crew flew under the flag of the United States, and headed out to sea. They soon spied a British ship, and the fight was on! Even though he was too young to handle the ship's guns or load the cannonballs, Forten worked with the other youths to carry gunpowder to the men for refilling their guns while they were shooting. Up and down the stairs of the ship he went, carrying gunpowder from belowdecks up to the men who were loading the guns. It was exciting but dangerous work. Both ships battled long and hard, but finally the British ship surrendered, signaling by lowering its flag. The Americans won!

Forten continued with the crew on the *Royal Louis*. Several weeks after their first battle, they saw another British ship. They sailed close by to attack, but soon found themselves surrounded by three British ships. It was a trap! The crew on the *Royal Louis* knew they could either sink or surrender. They lowered their American flag to surrender and became prisoners of the British.

For Forten, it was a frightening time. British sailors often sold African American prisoners into slavery. He and the other sailors were taken onto one of the British ships where they were inspected and the men were separated from the boys.

Forten and the younger boys were watched over by the British captain's son. They were given more freedom as prisoners than the men. One day, Forten and the other boys were playing a game of marbles. The British captain's son joined in, and he and James became friends.

The American prisoners were then taken to a prison ship to wait out the war. Instead of selling Forten as a slave, the captain let him get on the prison ship. Years later Forten said that playing marbles saved his life. Because he became friends with the captain's son during the game, the captain let him remain as a prisoner of war.

Two weeks after his ship was captured, news arrived that the Americans had won the Revolutionary War! Forten and the other prisoners were released from the prison ship. Forten returned home to Philadelphia and went into the sail-making business. He eventually became one of the wealthiest men in Philadelphia. He dedicated much of his life and money to helping African Americans experience the same freedom he fought bravely to win for the new country.

The Free African Society

The Revolutionary War was over. As the colonists in America were struggling to form a new country based on the idea that everyone was created equal, African Americans were very aware of the many ways they weren't being treated as equals. Thomas Jefferson, George Washington, and many of the men who wrote the Declaration of Independence and worked to start the new government in America owned slaves. Many laws that the new government wrote did not value the rights of African Americans, whether they were free or slaves. A large number of white colonists, however, spoke out against slavery.

On Thursday, April 12, 1787—more than a decade after the Declaration of Independence and two years before George Washington was elected president—the Free African Society was formed. Richard Allen and Absalom Jones, along with six other men, met in Philadelphia and took steps to form this first organization supporting African Americans. The Free African Society was a church, a place to help poor people, and began giving support to African Americans and other people who believed they should be free.

Groups like the Free African Society encouraged people to form other groups in cities such as Boston and New York. Churches for African Americans were started. Schools were built. African Americans formed new societies, such as the African Lodge No. 459 and the Boston African Society, to create an identity for themselves in America.

During the early years after the Revolutionary War, many African Americans who lived as free people were able to achieve very important accomplishments. Many of them also spoke out strongly against slavery. Groups such as the Free African Society formed a strong base of support for these individuals during this time.

The Forten Family of Philadelphia

At Lombard Street in Philadelphia, James and Charlotte Forten's house became a gathering place for family, friends, and antislavery leaders. Well-to-do because of the prosperous sail-making business that James owned, this couple opened their home to various generations of family members who were having financial troubles. They took in orphaned children whose parents had been close friends of the family. They had frequent guests stay for dinner, many of whom were famous leaders, both black and white, in the fight against slavery.

Both James and Charlotte were actively involved in improving daily life for free blacks, aiding runaway slaves on their journey to freedom, and influencing the government to bring an end to slavery. Charlotte, along with three of her daughters, was a charter member of the Philadelphia Female Anti-Slavery Society. Charlotte and James were both active members of their church. James organized and led meetings that pushed for equal rights for African Americans, both free and enslaved. He

Phillis Wheatley
(1753?-1784)

Phillis Wheatley arrived in America as a slave when she was just a child of seven or eight. Bought by John and Susannah Wheatley, she was raised more like a daughter than a slave. By the time Wheatley was 14, she started writing poetry. She wrote about religion and American patriots. When Wheatley traveled to England in 1773, her book of poetry was published and she became an instant celebrity among many American and European people. After the death of John and Susannah Wheatley in the late 1770s, Wheatley was given her freedom, but she died a few years later from ill health.

Play a Game of Marbles

The history of marbles goes back thousands of years. Some of the earliest marbles were made from stone or clay. Scientists have found marbles from ancient Rome and Egypt. These findings, as well as stories in ancient literature about the use of marbles, show us that the game of marbles has been popular for centuries. James Forten and other colonial Americans probably played with marbles made of baked clay. Glass marbles weren't very popular until the late 1800s, when a German glassblower invented the marble scissors that made glass marbles easier to make.

Materials

Adult supervision required

Oven-bake clay (found in craft
   stores)
Cookie sheet for baking
Sidewalk chalk

Preheat oven to 275°. To make the marbles, roll about ½ inch (1.3 cm) of clay, or almost the size of a penny, between the palms of your hands until a smooth ball is formed. Make about 20 small marbles and one larger marble, about 1 inch (1.3 cm), or the size of a quarter. Place the marbles on the cookie sheet, being careful not to flatten their sides. Bake for 15 minutes, according to the package instructions.

To play a game of marbles similar to the one James Forten and the captain's son played, draw a 1-foot-wide (30-cm-wide) circle on the ground. Draw a 5- to 7-foot-wide (1.5 to 2-m) circle around the first. Each player puts five small marbles at random in the middle ring. Players take turns shooting their larger marble from the outside ring and into the middle, trying to hit the smaller marbles. To shoot your large marble, cup your hand as shown in the illustration on page 44. Rest the marble on the edge of your cupped hand. Push the marble quickly with your thumb so it shoots out and into the middle ring. The player gets to keep any small marbles that are knocked out of the middle ring.

If a player knocks a marble out of the middle ring, the player gets to continue shooting from the place the larger marble stopped. If a player doesn't knock a marble out of the middle ring, then it is the next player's turn.

wrote and circulated many petitions that were presented to state and national legislatures. He stated his strong views about racial equality in a series of articles known as "Letters from a Man of Colour."

Together, James and Charlotte influenced the next two generations of the Forten family to become outstanding leaders of their city, state, and country. They gave their children an excellent education, even when public schools refused to admit them as students because of the color of their skin.

The oldest sons of James and Charlotte Forten continued their parents' fight against slavery. James Jr. and Robert worked at the sail-making loft with their father. James Jr. was much in demand to speak at antislavery meetings. Together with his brother Robert and brother-in-law Robert Purvis, James Jr. helped form the Young Men's Anti-Slavery Society of Philadelphia. Gifted with a fine voice, James Jr. sang at various meetings. His poems and articles appeared in antislavery newspapers.

Robert Forten and his wife Mary were members of several antislavery organizations. Robert also served on the Philadelphia Vigilant Committee with his brother-in-law Robert Purvis to help runaway slaves escape safely to freedom. A frequent lecturer at antislavery meetings, Robert returned from England to join the Union army when the Civil War began, but died shortly thereafter.

Margaretta, Harriet, and Sarah, the daughters of James and Charlotte Forten, grew up to be notable antislavery leaders. All three helped establish the Philadelphia Female Anti-Slavery Society and led various committees during the 36 years of this organization's existence. John Greenleaf Whittier was so impressed with the outstanding moral and leadership qualities of these sisters that he wrote a poem to them in their honor, "To the Daughters of James Forten."

Margaretta was a teacher and eventually opened up her own school. She was a strong advocate of women's rights as well as equal rights of all people. A secretary of the Philadelphia Female Anti-Slavery Society, she was selected to be on a committee to draft its constitution. After her father's death, her excellent skills as a businesswoman enabled her to help manage his huge estate for her mother and younger brothers.

Harriet married Robert Purvis, and together as a team they supported antislavery causes. Harriet devoted her time to raising their children, working in various leadership positions of the Philadelphia Female Anti-Slavery Society, and hosting well-known abolitionist leaders in their home. A skillful seamstress, she served on the sewing committee to help those who were less fortunate. Harriet and Robert supported the Free Produce Society, which refused to purchase items produced on plantations that had slave labor.

Sarah married Joseph Purvis, Robert Purvis's brother. She was a gifted poet. Her poems and essays often appeared in antislavery newspapers including the *Liberator*. She held many leadership positions in antislavery societies and was a frequent lecturer. She worked tirelessly to bring improvements in the education system and campaigned to bring an end to slavery.

Less is known about James and Charlotte's two youngest sons, Thomas and William. They both received an excellent education. William became active in politics and his name appears as one of the signers of a broadside calling free blacks to join the Union Army during the Civil War.

The Forten legacy continued with their grandchildren. One of the most famous was Charlotte Forten Grimké, the daughter of Robert and Mary Forten. Her diaries, still around today, reveal what it was like to grow up as a free black woman in America during the years just before the Civil War—in the midst of extreme racial tensions and prejudice.

Another one of Forten's grandchildren was Charles B. Purvis, the son of Harriet and Robert Purvis. He grew up to establish a successful medical career. A physician, teacher, and hospital administrator, he was also on the medical faculty of Howard University. With his appointment to the Freedmen's Hospital in 1881, he became the first African American to oversee a civilian hospital.

Write an Almanac

Even though they did not have the same rights as others, free African Americans such as Benjamin Banneker used their limited freedom to become educated and influential during America's growth.

Banneker lived on his family's tobacco farm near Baltimore, Maryland. One day a man gave him a pocket watch. Banneker took the watch apart and used it to make the first wooden clock ever built in America. With gears carved out of wood, this clock kept perfect time for more than 40 years. People came from miles away to see this wonder and the man who built it.

Banneker loved to study. He studied the stars, and stayed awake all night to watch their movements. He slept during the early part of the day, and did his work in the afternoon at a large table covered with books and papers.

President George Washington appointed Banneker to help a group of men map and measure the land that would become Washington, D.C. When the chief engineer suddenly left the project and took the detailed maps back to France, everyone thought the project would fail. But Banneker remembered every single detail on the plans and drew the map from memory! The project was a success.

Banneker used math along with astronomy, the study of the planets and stars, to predict important events in the future such as the sun's eclipse (say it: ih CLIPS). An eclipse occurs when the moon moves in front of the sun and totally blocks out the sun's light. It looks dark for a few hours even if it's the middle of the day.

For several years, Banneker used his astronomy and math skills to write almanacs, which are books farmers use for weather reports. His almanacs also included recipes, poems, medical advice, information about festivals and holidays, and articles against slavery.

Materials
Paper
Pen or pencil
Markers
Hole punch
Report folder

On the paper, keep an account of the weather in your area by checking the temperature, measuring the amount of rain or snow, and recording whether each day is sunny, windy, or stormy. Write down some of your favorite recipes. Draw pictures of holidays and festivals that take place in your town. Write poems or articles about things that are important to you. Collect all of these and put them in a report folder to make your almanac. If you want to share your almanac with others, photocopy the pages and make several folders to give to the people you know. Benjamin Banneker sent a copy of his almanac to President Thomas Jefferson. His almanacs sold throughout the 16 states in the Union and even in England.

Make a Star-Watching Chart

Benjamin Banneker loved astronomy. Many nights he headed out to a field on his farm, wrapped up in a blanket, and lay on the ground to study the night sky.

Materials

Tracing paper
Pen
Scissors
Paper plate, dessert-size
Glue
Blanket
Flashlight
Red cellophane, 4 inches (10 cm)
    square
Rubber band

Trace the small chart of stars onto a piece of paper. Cut out the chart and glue it to the paper plate so it's easy to hold. On the next clear night, grab a warm blanket. Take a flashlight and cover the lens with the piece of red cellophane held in place by a rubber band. This red light makes it easier for your eyes to see the stars and your chart at the same time.

Go outside to your backyard with a friend after the sky is dark enough to see the stars. Lie flat on your back, wrapped up in the blanket, and look at the stars. Try to find some of the constellations, or groups of stars, that Benjamin Banneker saw when he studied the night sky. Use your special flashlight to peek at your chart for the names of some of the brighter constellations. During different seasons of the year you will be able to see different groups of stars.

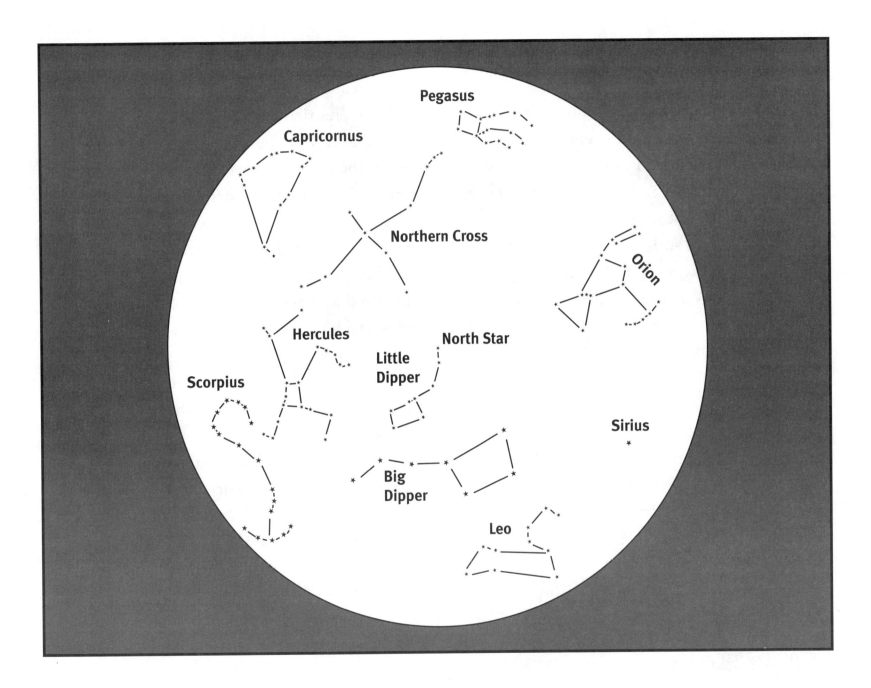

America's Founding Fathers

The cities of Philadelphia and Boston were seedbeds of liberty during the events surrounding the American Revolution. In Philadelphia, the Liberty Bell rang out time and time again announcing important meetings at Independence Hall and monumental events such as the signing of the Declaration of Independence. In Boston, freedom was talked about on every street corner and under every tree as the British soldiers came and occupied this important port city.

The spirit of liberty spread like wildfire among the colonists. Patriot leaders met and the Continental Congress was formed. These Founding Fathers signed their names to the Declaration of Independence and eventually drew up a Constitution to establish a new form of government during the birth of the United States of America.

There are no signatures of African American leaders on any of these documents. Why? The answer is simple. At that time, African Americans were not allowed to be elected as government officials. Most of the time, African Americans were not even allowed to vote. In some states, there were even restrictions placed on how far they were allowed to travel. They were not allowed to participate in the meetings where important decisions were made regarding the new government.

However, research has revealed that in the cities of Philadelphia and Boston, there were established communities of African Americans whose leaders interacted with the new leaders of the nation in influential ways. Their heroic actions, powerful use of petitions, fiery speeches, and organization of mass meetings influenced the governmental decisions being made behind doors that were closed to their attendance.

Because of their influence, the names of these outstanding African American leaders are now to be counted among the Founding Fathers. Richard Allen, Absalom Jones, and James Forten of Philadelphia along with Prince Hall and George Middleton of Boston are some of the key men who are remembered today alongside Thomas Jefferson and Benjamin Franklin as Founding Fathers of the United States of America.

Founding Fathers in Philadelphia

By far the most outstanding African American leader during the early years of our nation was Richard Allen from Philadelphia. A Frederick Douglass of his generation, this Founding Father used the pulpit as a platform to organize black America to be a powerful voice in the nation. Committed to meeting the spiritual needs and the personal needs of Philadelphia's black community—the largest in America at the time—as well as African Americans throughout the nation, Allen rose up to become a well-known leader highly respected by both blacks and whites alike.

Richard Allen was known as one of best preachers to ever stand behind a pulpit. He was a devout Methodist. His enthusiasm and passion for his faith drew large crowds. He became the founder of Bethel Church, the mother church of the African

Richard Allen
(1760-1831)

Born in the city of Philadelphia as a slave, Richard Allen eventually purchased his own freedom. After a religious experience, he dedicated his life to preaching. During the American Revolution, he drove wagonloads of salt from the shores of Delaware inland to the patriot troops, preaching to communities along his route. After the war, he was invited to move back to Philadelphia and preach to the black congregation at St. George's Methodist Episcopal Church. When Allen and his friends walked out of the church because of racism against them, they formed the Free African Society. As founder of the African Methodist Episcopal (AME) Church, Richard Allen became the denomination's first bishop. A strong abolitionist, civil rights activist, and community leader, Allen became president of the First Negro National Convention.

The Liberty Bell became a symbol of freedom and equal rights for African Americans during the years following the American Revolution.

Methodist Episcopal (AME) Church, and was appointed as its first bishop.

Ever concerned for his fellow African Americans, Richard Allen organized and led benevolent societies, mutual aid societies, and moral societies to help struggling free blacks and fugitive slaves in the community of Philadelphia. His leadership inspired similar helpful organizations to be established in black communities throughout the country.

When a yellow fever epidemic broke out in 1793, the mayor of Philadelphia contacted Richard Allen and his friend Absalom Jones. The mayor asked them to organize men and women to help with the unpleasant and overwhelming task of dealing with the more than 5,000 deaths that occurred. In spite of the danger, Allen and Jones worked side by side with their friend Dr. Benjamin Rush to supply medical treatment for the sick, and to bury the dead.

When the War of 1812 brought threats of invasion to Philadelphia from British troops, government officials again called on Allen and his fellow leaders to help. Richard Allen, Absalom Jones, and James Forten organized the Black Legion, a regiment of 2,500 soldiers who stood guard to protect the city until the threats went away.

Sarah Allen
(1764-1849)

A former slave, Sarah married Richard Allen, who purchased her freedom. Most of her time was devoted to raising their six children and being actively involved in the AME Church in Philadelphia where her husband was founder, preacher, and first bishop of the denomination. Fondly known by the members of her congregation as "Mother Allen," she helped form the Daughters of Conference. This society provided financial assistance, food, and clothing to needy ministers of its denomination. As agents along the Underground Railroad, Sarah Allen and her husband frequently opened their home to help fugitive slaves escaping to freedom.

Citizenship and equal rights were important to Richard Allen. When the American Colonization Society (ACS) threatened to send free blacks away from America to resettle in Liberia, Allen organized a huge protest meeting at Bethel Church. Demanding their right to stay as citizens in America, the country of their birth, Richard Allen led the fight. Allen wrote articles that were published in various abolitionist papers declaring that the ACS was trying to get rid of free blacks in hopes of establishing slavery as an even stronger institution. He circulated petitions calling for the end of slavery, submitting these to both the state and national governments.

In 1830, Allen organized and was president of the American Society of Free Persons of Color, the first national convention for African Americans. Delegates from various states attended. For the first time in history, a national network was established to help both free and enslaved blacks stand up and fight for their rights.

Over the years, he often worked side-by-side with his close friend Absalom Jones. Born into slavery, Jones was able to purchase freedom for his wife and himself through years of hard work and savings. A founding member of the St. Thomas African Episcopal Church, Jones became the first African American Episcopal priest in the United States. Well-known for his speaking skills, Absalom Jones also believed in education as a way to improve life for African Americans. He founded a school at his church for children from African American families in Philadelphia who were denied entrance into the city's public schools. Jones devoted the last years of his life to joining Richard Allen in the fight against the ACS efforts to transport free blacks to live in Africa.

The third leader in this powerful trio from Philadelphia was James Forten, the wealthy sail maker. As a Founding Father, Forten's name appeared often at the forefront in the fight for equal rights, equal education, and equal citizenship for all African Americans—both in Philadelphia and throughout the emerging nation. When James Forten died, his funeral was one of the largest Philadelphia had ever seen. Whites and blacks alike crowded the street to pay tribute to this outstanding leader in their community.

Founding Fathers in Boston

A former slave, Prince Hall owned a leather shop in Boston called the Golden Fleece. As a first step toward organization, Hall and his fellow leaders of the African American community in Boston decided to join the Masons. Denied membership by the colonial groups, Prince Hall and 14 other free blacks joined the Free and Accepted Masons on March 6, 1775, as part of the British troops stationed in Boston. Hall and his group were given a permit to continue meeting after the British left Boston. African Lodge Number 1 was given the new number 459 when it was officially chartered in London in 1787. The lodge's first grand master was Prince Hall. After his death, the members voted to rename it the Prince Hall Grand Lodge in memory of their beloved founder and leader.

Deeply concerned that slavery still flourished in a society thirsty for freedom, Hall and eight other black Bostonians signed a petition calling for equal rights and the end of slavery. Another petition started by Hall called for the release of three free blacks who had been kidnapped and sold into slavery. His petition moved Governor John Hancock to ensure their return to Boston.

As a leader in Boston's African American community, Prince Hall was concerned that children of voting and tax-paying free black citizens such as himself were not allowed in the public schools. When his protests fell on deaf ears, Hall opened up a school in his own home to provide a solid education for children from African American families who lived in Boston.

As a Founding Father, Prince Hall was instrumental in helping bring an end to slavery in the colony of Massachusetts in 1783 and an end to the American transatlantic slave trade in 1808, a year after his death.

Joseph Cinque
(1811-1852)

On the *Amistad*, a ship carrying kidnapped Africans from Africa to Cuba, Joseph Cinque led 53 other slaves in a revolt that captured the ship and its crew. Their ship was later captured at Long Island in New York by another ship whose crew wanted to force Cinque and his men to remain in slavery. The Coast Guard boarded Cinque's ship, and news spread throughout New York about the Africans' situation. Members of the abolitionist movement who wanted to end slavery then stepped in to help Cinque and his men by taking this case to court. It eventually reached the United States Supreme Court, where former President John Quincy Adams argued for the slaves' freedom from slavery. They won, and were allowed to return home to Africa.

George Middleton was another leader in Boston. This Founding Father organized and led an all-black unit during the American Revolution called the Bucks of America. He became one of the leading members of Prince Hall's Masonic lodge, eventually being elected as the third grand master after Hall's death. Over the years, Middleton worked closely with Prince Hall, his fellow leader and friend. Their names appear on various petitions and documents together.

Middleton and Hall organized and led the African Benevolent Society, which offered financial and legal help to African Americans in their community. Middleton joined Hall in his committed crusade for the end of slavery and equal rights for the black citizens of Boston. George Middleton also opened his home on Beacon Hill to important political gatherings. His house is a historical landmark in Boston today.

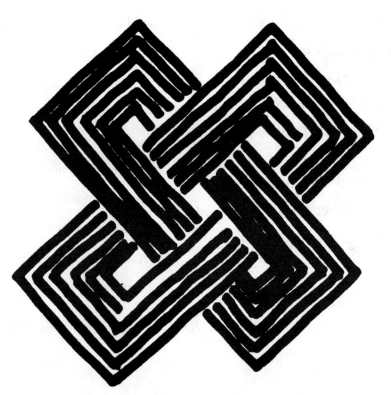

Kneeling Slave Medallion

Materials

Illustration of the medallion

Paper

Pencil

Glue

Poster board

Compass

Scissors

Cotton household string

Aluminum foil

Clear tape

Fine-tipped permanent marker

Many groups formed in America and other countries to speak out against slavery. Because of their efforts, Congress decided that the slave trade must end. On March 2, 1807, Congress passed a law that made it illegal to bring shiploads of captured Africans to America after January 1, 1808.

Even though the Atlantic slave trade officially ended, the fight still continued to abolish the institution of slavery in America. In London, Josiah Wedgwood designed a picture of a praying slave. This picture became a famous symbol for the groups who tried to end slavery. People made this picture into medallions and buttons. They had the picture sewn on their clothes and printed on items such as handheld fans.

Trace the picture of the praying man, and glue the picture to a piece of poster board. Using your compass, draw an 8-inch circle (20-cm) around this figure and cut it out. Spread a thin line of glue along

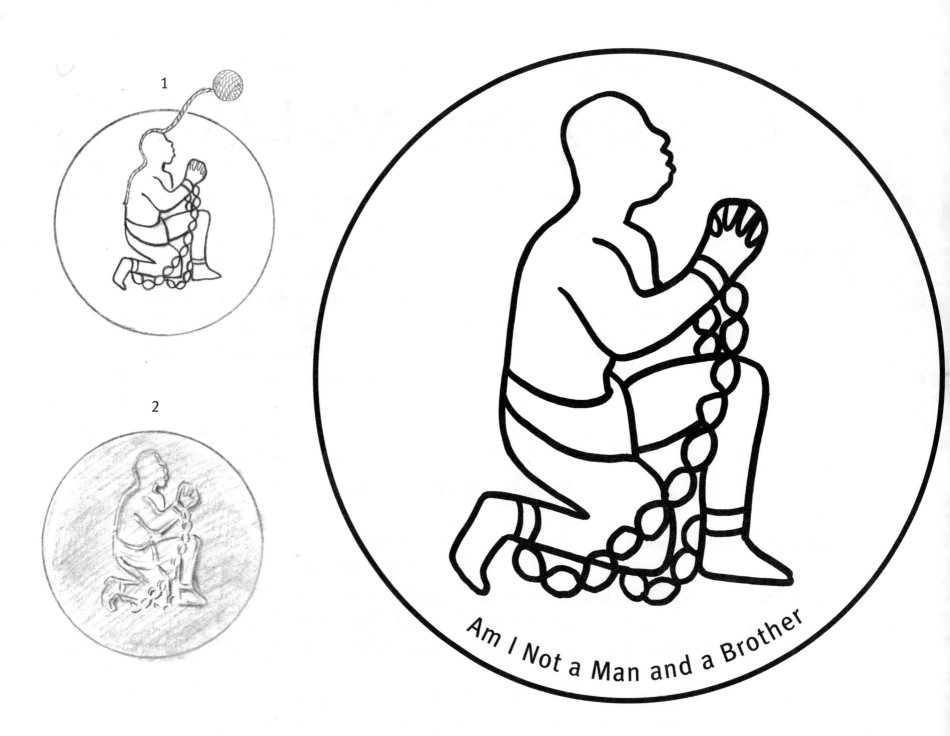

1

2

Am I Not a Man and a Brother

the outline of the praying man. Glue lengths of string along these lines. When the glue has dried, cover the design on the poster board with a large square of aluminum foil, wrapping the edges of foil to the back.

Tape the foil in place across the back. On the front of the medallion, use your thumb to gently rub the foil over the string so that the outline of the praying man becomes clear. Use a fine-tipped permanent marker to write across the bottom of the medallion, "Am I not a man and a brother?"

A Foundation of Faith

A traveling preacher after he obtained his freedom, Richard Allen was invited to preach early in the morning to the black congregation at St. George's Methodist Episcopal Church in Philadelphia, the city where he was born into slavery. Soon African Americans from Philadelphia flocked to St. George's to hear Allen's powerful preaching early each Sunday morning. The white members of the congrega-tion attended the main service later in the day.

One day, Richard Allen, Absalom Jones, and their friends joined the white members of the con-gregation and attended the main service at St. George's, as they usually did. On this Sunday, how-ever, they were directed away from the main sanc-tuary and told to sit upstairs in the newly built bal-cony. As they knelt in prayer by their seats in the balcony, one of the ushers pulled Absalom Jones to his feet and ordered him to move to the back of the balcony. When the prayer was over, Richard Allen, Absalom Jones, and the entire group of African Americans stood up and walked out of the church, expressing their protest over such unjust treatment.

Because of this incident, Richard Allen and his friends organized the Free African Society, a group that encouraged the spiritual growth and moral qualities of its members as well as provided finan-cial assistance to those in need. Committed to his Methodist beliefs, Allen went on to establish Bethel Church in Philadelphia. Bethel became the mother church of the African Methodist Episcopal

(AME) church, influencing church plants in every state of the nation and as far away as Haiti and Liberia.

Absalom Jones had different religious views than his close friend Richard Allen. Jones decided to join as a member in the Episcopal Church, eventually becoming the pastor of Saint Thomas's African Episcopal Church. In 1804, Absalom Jones rose to the position as the denomination's first black American priest.

In response to the restrictions and harsh treatment placed on black church members, many African Americans began to gather as a group in their own churches where they could sit where they chose, make decisions about their services, and worship more freely. In New York City, Peter Williams Sr. organized services for what eventually became the mother church of the African Methodist Episcopal Zion (AMEZ) Church.

Women took an active part in church life during the early years of the nation. In the early 1800s, Jarena Lee became a traveling evangelist for the AME church, preaching and holding prayer meetings across the northeastern United States. Catherine Ferguson started a Sunday School in New York City, helping children who were poor and homeless.

Because of the existence of slavery, conditions were difficult across the South, but religious leaders such as George Liele and Andrew Bryan preached to congregations as often as they could. Under Bryan's leadership, the First African Baptist Church was established in Savannah, Georgia, in the late 1700s.

3
Life on a Plantation

Plantations, or large farms found in the South, influenced the entire identity of the United States. Large crops of rice, tobacco, sugar, and cotton were grown on plantations and shipped to all corners of the world, establishing America as an important and strong country.

African Americans who were forced to work as slaves on these huge plantations might not have been aware of the impact their hard work had on the world, but they helped build America. African Americans have been a major force in the development of America, from its very beginnings as a young country to its success as a world power today.

Life on a plantation was difficult for African Americans living in slavery. They were often treated as if they had no feelings or personal rights. Many times conditions were harsh and terrifying, with threats of violent punishment or death being a part of everyday life. The constant fear of being sold or separated from beloved family members filled their thoughts.

Field workers had to work very hard from sunrise until sunset, with just a short break for lunch. Sometimes they even worked late into the night by lantern light. House workers worked long hours doing such jobs as cooking in hot kitchens or washing endless amounts of clothes by hand.

Norbert Rillieux
(1806-1894)

Plantations in Louisiana grew sugarcane. Through a lengthy and dangerous process called the "Jamaica Train," enslaved African Americans refined the sugarcane to produce sugar on plantations near New Orleans. However, sugar at this time was brownish and moist. Because of its expensive, slow-refining process, sugar was only eaten by the wealthy.

Born free in New Orleans, Norbert Rillieux (say it: RILL-ee) was the son of an African American enslaved mother and a wealthy white plantation owner and engineer. Recognizing his great intelligence, his father sent Rillieux to Paris to study engineering. Determined to improve the conditions of the "Jamaica Train," Rillieux spent many years designing a new way to process sugar by evaporation that produced sweet white crystals. This process revolutionized the sugar industry, making the United States known as the best manufacturer of sugar in the world. This evaporation process was also used to make condensed milk, soap, and glue. After living again in America, where his system was installed on plantations throughout Louisiana, Rillieux returned to Paris to become headmaster at his former school.

Twice a year, workers were given clothes made of rough material to wear. On some plantations, men were given two shirts, a pair of pants, and a jacket. Women were given six yards of wool fabric, six yards of cotton fabric, a needle, thread, and six buttons. Children were sometimes only given a long shirt to wear as a dress until they were six or seven years old, and were considered big enough to work in the fields.

Usually families lived in cabins set in rows called the quarters. Many people might live in each small cabin. Each cabin held mattresses stuffed with cornhusks and sometimes a few chairs or a table.

These cabins were set at a distance from the big houses where plantation owners lived. Spreading out from the big house were fields and gardens. In the gardens grew sweet potatoes or watermelons.

The fields were filled with cotton, corn, rice, or tobacco.

A large plantation was like its own town. Each plantation had its own factory for handling the cotton or other crops, its own system of law and order, and its own workers such as blacksmiths and carpenters. There was often a separate house for cooking, stables for the mules and horses, corn cribs to hold the corn, and a cotton gin to clean the cotton.

Food on a Plantation

The food African Americans were given during slavery often wasn't very good. On some plantations, the food was cooked in the main kitchen. The leftovers might be sent to the field workers. On other plantations, the workers were given a weekly measurement of corn and bacon and were expected to eat for the whole week from this small amount. They were also expected to cook their own meals after an exhausting day. Sometimes they made hoecakes by cooking a corn-meal batter on a hot hoe while they worked in the fields. A late supper was made over an open fire in a large black pot or in a big skillet.

Sometimes, slave families were given small garden plots. Slaves spent time after long work hours in the garden, trying to grow sweet potatoes, greens, corn, and watermelon. They would fish and trap raccoons, opossums, or turtles for extra meat.

Sometimes, but not often, they were able to keep a pig or several chickens.

Because corn was one of their main foods, African Americans cooked it in many different ways. They worked hard to create tasty ways to eat the kinds of food they had.

Grits

4 servings

Adult supervision required

Ingredients

4 cups (1 l) water

1 cup (160 g) grits

Salt and pepper to taste

Syrup, gravy, or eggs

Utensils

Measuring cups

Saucepan
Whisk

Put the water in the saucepan, and bring to a boil. Slowly add the grits. Turn the heat down low. Stir constantly with the whisk for about five minutes until the grits are thick. (Or follow the directions on the package.) Add salt and pepper.

Grits may be served at breakfast with syrup, gravy, or eggs.

Fried Mush

4 servings

Adult supervision required

Ingredients

4 cups water

1 cup cornmeal

Salt to taste

Butter to grease the loaf pan

Butter or bacon grease for frying

Syrup

Utensils

Measuring cups

Saucepan

Whisk

Glass loaf pan

Table knife

Heavy skillet

Metal turner

Put the water in the saucepan, and bring to a boil. Slowly add the cornmeal. Turn the heat down low. Stir constantly with the whisk for about five minutes until the cornmeal is thick.

Pour the cooked cornmeal into a greased loaf pan and allow to cool. Put it in the refrigerator overnight.

In the morning, take the cornmeal out of the loaf pan. Slice into ½-inch slices. Fry each slice in the skillet with a small amount of grease. Turn the slices over and continue to fry until both sides are crispy. Serve on a plate with syrup.

Greens

Dandelions grew wild in the yards and fields on plantations. They were a free source of green vegetables that tasted good when cooked with bacon grease. Dandelion leaves were picked fresh when they were young and tender, before the flowers had formed. Sometimes collards or spinach was grown in a small garden plot and harvested to make greens instead.

4 servings
Adult supervision required
Ingredients
2 quarts (2 l) fresh dandelion greens
   (other fresh greens may be
   substituted)
4 slices bacon
2 tablespoons (30 ml) minced onion
1 tablespoon (15 ml) vinegar
Salt
Pepper
Utensils
Serving bowl
Skillet
Metal spatula
Measuring spoons

Wash the greens well. Tear the greens into small pieces and put them into a serving bowl.

Fry the bacon in a skillet over low heat. Add the minced onions and cook until the bacon is crisp, chopping it into pieces with the metal spatula. Stir in the vinegar, salt, and pepper.

Pour the bacon mixture over the greens. Allow to cool before eating.

Juba

Juba (say it: JOO-buh) was a term that was used in a variety of ways. One of the most common meanings for the word *juba* was leftovers. Many African American families were given cuttings from vegetables, the ends of the meat, or crusts from bread. When cooking a meal, they would mix these leftovers together and try to make a tasty dish.

There also was a dance called the juba that used different clapping rhythms and a variety of dance steps. This dance became very popular in New Orleans. African Americans could be seen performing it in groups on the streets or at festivals. A later variation came to be known as the Charleston.

Some African Americans were given the name Juba. A person who was a skilled musician or dancer might be called Juba. In the African language of Bantu the word *juba* also meant to pat or keep rhythm. In many African languages, Juba was also a name for a child born on Monday. It was a common name given to girls. Children born into African American families were sometimes named Juba.

Make up your own rhymes and motions and clapping rhythms to go along with the words in this song. As you do, others can join along. Slap your thighs, clap your hands, snap your fingers, and jump up and down. Try speeding up the rhythm until you play Juba as fast as you can! As you shout and play this lively rhyming game with its verse describing leftovers, you will be reminded of the traditional game children played many years ago.

Juba

Juba this and juba that,
(clap)
And Juba killed a yellow cat.
(clap, clap)
You sift a meal, you give me the husk,
(clap)
You cook the bread, you give me the crust.
(clap, clap)
You fry the meat, you give me the skin,
(clap)
And that's where my mama's troubles begin.

(clap, clap)
Then you juba,
You just juba.
Juba up, juba down.
Juba all around the town.
Juba for ma, juba for pa,
Juba for your brother-in-law.
Juba that and juba this.
I'll keep rhyming, I won't miss.

Brer Rabbit and His Friends

African Americans were often forced to stay near their cabins after working hours so the owners of the plantations could maintain a guarded watch over them. African Americans who lived on plantations therefore developed ways to relax and have fun within the boundaries of their restricted activities. These forms of recreation often drew from their heritage. They played clapping games, danced, and made music that was a combination of the games, dances, and music which many had experienced in Africa. As children were born on the plantations, family members taught these games and dances to the younger generation.

One way to pass the time and help ease their troubles was to share stories about a much-loved trickster named Brer Rabbit. Brer Rabbit, even though he was a small animal, always managed to outsmart the larger animals such as Brer Fox and Brer Bear. Trickster tales had been common in Africa, and in America, Brer Rabbit tales became symbolic of the slaves and their relationship with their masters. People loved to hear stories about how Brer Rabbit used his common sense and quick wit to always make any situation turn to his advantage.

Read through the following tale. It reminds us of the tales heard in the slave quarters during quiet Sunday afternoons or Saturday evenings, when most enslaved African Americans were allowed to take a break from working. Families sat on the porch step, where a group of children would listen to a grown-up telling stories. You can share this tale by reading it aloud to your friends.

Brer Rabbit and Brer Pig

Now Brer Rabbit had a neighbor and that neighbor's name was Brer Pig. But Brer Pig didn't look like you see him today. Brer Pig was spotted and fat and smelled a lot like he does now, but his nose was different. Yessir, Brer Pig's nose was just as long and stretchy as an elephant's nose, and that's a fact.

Being neighborly and all, Brer Rabbit liked to visit his neighbor, except when it came time for

dinner. Now there never was anyone for miles around who was as greedy as Brer Pig, and it just bothered Brer Rabbit, his greediness and all.

Why, just last week when Brer Rabbit went to visit Brer Pig, it was dinner time. And just when the food was served and the corn was thrown over the fence, Brer Pig stuffed that corn into his mouth with his long stretchy nose, every single bite of it, before Brer Rabbit even had a chance to open his mouth. Imagine!

So Brer Rabbit went to the Good Lord to have a talk about his greedy neighbor. Brer Rabbit invited the Good Lord to come see for himself how greedy Brer Pig was with his long, stretchy elephant's nose. And when the Good Lord saw how things were going on, he just knew he'd have to do something. So he picked up Brer Pig out of his pen and chopped off his nose with a hatchet, clear up close to his mouth. And that's how come his nose is flat and square like, different from anyone else's.

Now when Brer Rabbit heard the Good Lord had taken things into his own hands, he invited himself to Brer Pig's again for dinner. Sure enough, when the corn was thrown over the fence, Brer Pig ran up to get it. But Brer Rabbit, seeing how things had changed, walked up just as casual as could be, and took his share of the dinner. Brer Pig, greedy as he was, dug around on the ground with his nose to get that corn, but he couldn't take all of it on account of his flat nose, so he just sort of grunted his way through the meal. This suited Brer Rabbit and his full stomach just fine. In fact, being neighborly and all, Brer Rabbit often had dinner with Brer Pig from that day on.

Story Starters

Use these story starters, based on popular Brer Rabbit tales, to make up stories of your own. All it takes is a little imagination—and a love for that trickster Brer Rabbit.

Brer Rabbit and the Ripe Grapes

Now Brer Rabbit had a girl, and oh did his heart flutter each and every time he thought of her!

Why, it seemed like he had dinner at her place almost every night he could. But there was just one problem. Brer Fox liked the same girl, too.

One day, as Brer Rabbit sat by the side of the road thinking of how to fix this problem, along came Brer Fox. "Where are you going?" Brer Rabbit asked, just as casual as you please.

"To my girl's for dinner," Brer Fox said.

Well, just then, Brer Rabbit took to remembering a bunch of ripe grapes he'd found next to a hornet's nest in the woods. And he knew how much Brer Fox loved ripe grapes and . . .

Brer Rabbit Finds Some Meat

Now one day Brer Rabbit was walking along the road, whistling as bright as the sunshine. And there, right smack-dab in front of his nose, was some tasty-looking meat hanging from the branch of a tree. But before Brer Rabbit could say the word, "Dinner," up walked Brer Bear.

"Dinner!" Brer Bear said, licking his lips.

"Sure enough," Brer Rabbit agreed. "Why, there's dinner enough here for the both of us for three weeks running."

Brer Bear started reaching out with his big bear claws when suddenly Brer Rabbit said, "Wait!" Brer Rabbit tapped his toe, thinking. "If we start eating now, we'll be too tired to carry the leftovers home when our meal is done. How about if you run off and grab a couple of buckets for us to carry everything home in?"

Brer Bear took off lickety split for those buckets, but as soon as he turned the corner, Brer Rabbit . . .

Tell Me a Riddle

Another way enslaved African Americans found recreation that drew from their heritage was to tell riddles. Riddle tales were common in Africa, and they became a well-known source of entertainment for African American families on plantations after they had finished a hard week in the fields. Often, these riddles didn't really have a simple answer that made a lot of sense. Instead, they were springboards for many interesting conversations while sitting together on the porch on a hot summer's evening.

After you read these riddles and guess their answers, try making up some riddles of your own.

Riddle: What walks for miles and miles every day, but then hides under the bed at night?
Answer: A shoe.

Riddle: What's this? You're happy when you don't have it and if someone wanted to give it to you, you wouldn't take it for all the money in the world.
Answer: A sickness.

Riddle: What has 3 legs up with 14 legs down and goes from place to place, just like everything's as normal as can be?
Answer: A man riding his mule. Now the man has two legs, and the mule has four legs. That makes six. The man's two hounds are following him, and they each have four legs. That makes 14 legs down. And if the man is carrying a three-legged milking stool upside down on his head, why that makes three legs up, then, doesn't it?

Children's Rhymes

Childhood was very brief for children born into slavery. Often, the children's mothers had to work in the field during the day, so one woman might be in charge of watching a group of small children. This woman was usually called "Aunty." She kept the young children with her through the day, playing games and caring for them. They played games such as marbles, jump rope, and tag. These games were little tastes of freedom that didn't last long.

Children were put to work at a very young age, as soon as they could pick up rocks out of the field or carry water in a bucket to thirsty workers. By the time they were 10 or older, they were forced to do steady work in the field or in the house.

When children were born, a page from a newspaper might be saved in the family Bible to keep track of the special day, even though few knew how to read.

This Little Piggy

Babies were loved and cherished. This rhyme was a favorite to say while playing with a baby. It was used to count the baby's toes or fingers. Each finger or toe was wiggled in turn as each little piggy was described.

This little piggy wants some corn.
This little piggy says, "Where you going to get it from?"
This little piggy says, "Out of Massa's barn."
This little pig says, "Run go tell!"
This little pig says, "Twee, twee, twee, I'll tell old
*   Massa, tell old Massa!"*

Bessie Jones and Bess Lomax Hawes, *Step It Down*. Athens, GA.: University of Georgia Press, 1987.

Engine Rubber Number Nine

This nonsense rhyme was said while clapping hands. It was also used to count off players before a game to choose someone to be "it."

One person should stand in front of a group of children. As the person chants the rhyme, she points to each child. On the last word of the rhyme, the child she pointed at comes over and joins her. She repeats the rhyme again until all the children except one are standing with her in a group. The last person called is "it."

Engine rubber number nine
Stick your head in turpentine.
Turpentine will make you shine,
Engine rubber number nine.

Step It Down

Children's Songs

Music was an important part of life for children of enslaved African Americans. As with all children, games were made more fun by adding songs. Often, children living in slavery saw and heard their master's children singing songs and playing games. They would sing these songs and play these games, too, adding verses and rhythms that drew from their daily experiences living on a plantation.

Little Sally Walker

This was a fun song that could be sung with a group of children on a quiet afternoon.

One child sits in the center of a ring of children. While the children standing in a circle sing the song, the child in the center acts out the words. After each verse of the song is chanted or sung, the child in the center chooses a new person to sit in the middle and act out the words to the song. Sing the song until everyone has a turn.

Little Sally Walker,
Sitting in a saucer,
Crying and a-weeping over all she have done.
Oh, rise up on your feet,
Oh, wipe your cheeks,
Oh, turn to the east,
Oh, turn to the west,
Oh, turn to the very one that you love the best.
Oh, shake it to the east,
Oh, shake it to the west,
Oh, shake it to the very one that you love the best.

Step It Down

76

Hambone

This is a lively song. There are many verses that can be added to the description of the wedding feast.

The persons chanting or singing the song can alternately pat their thighs and their chests, back and forth, in a quick rhythm that accents the words. In a quieter version, this song was sung as a lullaby to put babies or young children to sleep.

Hambone, Hambone, what did you do?
I got a train and I fairly flew.
Hambone, Hambone, where did you go?
I hopped up to Miss Lucy's door.
I asked Miss Lucy would she marry me.
(in falsetto) "Well, I don't care if Papa don't care!"
First come in was Mister Snake,
He crawled all over that wedding cake.
Next walked in was Mister Tick,
He ate so much that it made him sick.
Next walked in was Mister Coon,
We asked him to sing us a wedding tune.
Now Ham- . . .
Now Ham- . . .

Step It Down

Thomas Green Bethune (1849-1908)

Blind from birth, Thomas Green was sold as an infant with his enslaved parents to Colonel Bethune in Georgia. When Thomas Green was four years old, Colonel Bethune bought a piano for his daughters. Listening to the girls practice daily, young Thomas sat down one day at the piano and played several tunes perfectly!

Realizing his talent and genius, the Bethune family began hiring Thomas out to play piano for concerts and social gatherings. He became known as Blind Tom. Eventually, he practiced eight hours a day and knew how to play at least 5,000 songs, including selections from Bach, Beethoven, and Chopin. His brilliant musical ability is thought to have earned his master over $100,000. After the Civil War, Thomas Green Bethune chose to remain under the care of the Bethune family until his death.

Children's Games

Many games played by African American children during this time were played for fun. Many games were noncompetitive. Here are some games of the time for you to try.

Skip to the Barbershop

This skipping game was played by a group of children. Everyone got a turn to skip across the room, often trying to be the one who could skip the best.

To play this game, all players line up along one side of the room. On the other side of the room, place different articles of clothing, one for each child. As the children recite the rhyme in unison, one child is chosen to skip across the room and bring the piece of clothing back that is mentioned in the verse. Repeat the rhyme until each player has a turn to skip across the room and back.

Skip, skip, to the barbershop,
I left my hat at the barbershop
And three sticks of candy.

One for you, one for me,
And one for sister Sally.
Skip, skip, to the barbershop,
I left my coat at the barbershop, etc.

Step It Down

William, William, Trembletoe

This was a popular game to play. The children all sat in a circle and each held one hand toward the center of the circle. If there were a small number of children in the circle, all the fingers of each child's hand were counted. If there were a large number of children in the circle, they just counted the pointer finger on one hand of each child. You can play this game, too!

Choose a leader to stand in the center of your circle of players. All the players stick their hands out toward the center of the circle. The leader counts the number of fingers. Everyone can recite the rhyme in unison until the last person is chosen to go out at the end of the rhyme. This chosen person hides in the corner or around the side of a building. The rest of the players in the circle should then each pick the name of an object to name themselves such as a house, cow, elephant, or spoon. Whisper these names to the leader. Choose one extra name for the person hiding in the corner.

The leader then calls to the person hiding in the corner, "What do you want to come home on?" The leader lists all the names the players chose for themselves, plus the extra name. If the person guesses the extra name, she has to return to the circle on tiptoe. If the person guesses one of the other player's names, that player gets up and brings her back to the circle.

After the player has returned to the circle, you can choose a new leader and start the game all over again! Notice that there really isn't a "winner" to this game.

William, William, Trembletoe
He's a good fisherman to catch them hens,
Put 'em in the pens.

Some lays eggs; some don't.
Wire, briar, limberlock
Set and sing till twelve o'clock.
The clock fell down,
The mouse ran around.
Y-O-U-T spells OUT.

Step It Down

Old Grey Horse!

This was a simple game to play with popcorn or peanuts. Each player starts out with the same number of pieces of popcorn or peanuts in separate bowls. One player starts the game by holding out an unknown number of popcorn pieces or peanuts in his closed fist. Then he recites the rhyme, taking the part of the first player. If another player (who recites the second player's lines in turn) guesses the correct number of popcorn pieces or peanuts held in the person's hand, that player wins those pieces and can add them to his bowl. If a player guesses too many or too few, that player has to give the popcorn- or peanut-holding player the number of popcorn pieces or peanuts to make up the difference between the guess and the actual number. If you play with more than two players, take turns guessing and reciting with the player sitting to your right. The player who ends up with all the pieces of popcorn or peanuts wins the game.

First Player: Old grey horse!
Second Player: I'll ride him!
First Player: How many miles?
Second Player: (Guess a number.)

Step It Down

Sew a Doll

Children played with dolls. They carried their dolls with them, pretending to feed and take care of them, and at night, dolls offered comfort as children held them in their arms. A doll might be made from a flour sack and stuffed with scraps of cotton from the field. If there were old clothes that could be cut up and used for fabric, a dress could be made for the doll to wear.

Materials

Man's cotton sock, tan or brown
Scissors
Needle
Thread
Ruler
Cotton balls, jumbo-sized
Cotton dress fabric, about 8 by 12
    inches (20 by 30 cm)

Cut the sock into two pieces as shown so that the straight piece is at least 8 inches (20 cm) long. Use a needle and thread to make tiny stitches across one open edge of the straight piece. Turn this inside out to form the doll's body. Stuff the body with the cotton balls as you sew the bottom closed.

Roll the heel up lengthwise to form a long log or tube. Stitch along the length of this tube to sew it closed. This will be the arms. Attach the arms to the body by stitching the tube across the back of the body about 2½ inches (6 cm) below the top of the head.

To make the dress for the doll, fold the rectangle of cotton dress fabric in half to form a 6 by 8-inch (15 by 20-cm) rectangle. Stitch up the 8-inch (20-cm) side edge, leaving the top and bottom open. Position this stitched seam along the center back of the dress. Cut two 1-inch (2.5-cm) armholes along the sides of the dress, about 2 inches (5 cm) down from the top edge. Slip the dress over the doll's head and pull the arms through the armholes.

Use the needle and a knotted thread to make a widely spaced stitch around the top edge of the dress, starting at the back seam and going around the front and the back again. This stitch should be about 1 inch (2.5 cm) down from the top of the dress and parallel to the top edge. Pull the thread tightly from the knot to gather the dress around the neck of the doll. Stitch this thread to the doll's back, attaching the dress at this point. Make another knot, cut the thread, and your doll is ready!

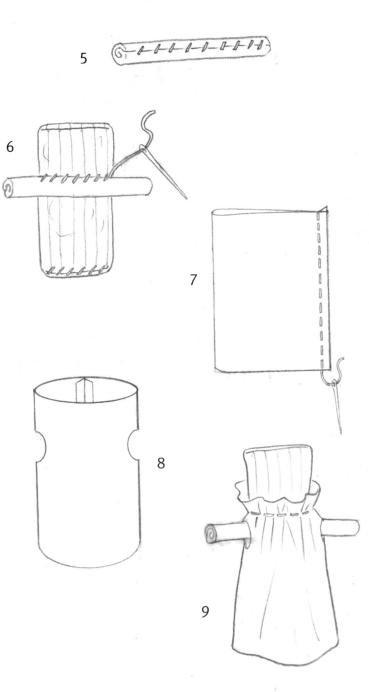

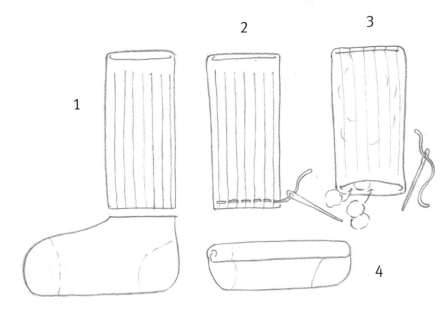

Hoop and Stick

Children living in the slave quarters didn't have many toys. They played outdoors when they had a chance. Their toys were often made from sticks, rocks, or scraps of fabric. One toy children liked to play with on the plantations was a large hoop made from a thin strip of wood or a metal hoop from a broken barrel. They rolled the hoop along the ground, trying to make it balance and stay upright by guiding it with a short stick they held in one hand.

Materials
Hula hoop
Short stick or ruler
Large, flat playing area

Stand the hoop up and give it one push with your hand. Run along beside the hoop. Hold the short stick in your other hand, guiding the hoop along its outside rim. Only use the stick to guide your hoop and keep it balanced, no hands allowed! If your hoop falls down, pick it up and give it another push to start the game over again.

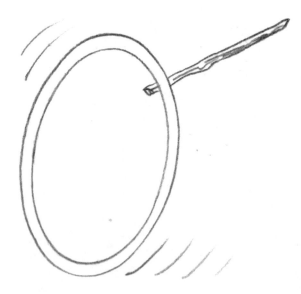

Artistic Crafts

There were enslaved African Americans who worked in pottery factories in South Carolina. Some of these potters created a very curious and unusual form of jug. Face Vessels, as these jugs were called, were clay jars in the shape of human faces. Some were teeny tiny and measured only inches tall. Others were quite large and stood almost two feet (61 cm) high. Most Face Vessels had large eyes and big teeth. These fascinating art forms demonstrated the creative spirit of the potters who made them.

Basket weavers created baskets in a variety of shapes for a number of different uses. On rice plantations, skilled workers wove sturdy baskets called fanners. These were used to winnow (say it: WIN-oh) the rice, a process where the rough part of the plant was separated from the grain of rice. This particular type of basket weaving had its origins in Africa, where there is a long history of planting and harvesting rice.

Music and Rhythm

Music and rhythm were very important to African Americans who lived on plantations. While working through the long, hard days, they sang songs. Some of their songs were filled with a rhythm that helped them pick cotton or work machines at the right speed. Some of their songs had words with hidden meanings, such as directions for following the Underground Railroad (a secret escape route for runaway slaves), calls for joining a revolt, or details about an upcoming secretly held church meeting. Some of their songs were songs of faith and helped encourage them.

In the evenings or during the time they weren't required to work, music was a way to remember the importance of their musical heritage from Africa and to pass this heritage down to their children. Drums, especially, were used both as a form of recreation and as a way to beat out secret messages to African Americans living on nearby plantations. Drums had been used to send messages in Africa in a similar way. Some plantation owners encouraged the use of drums, music, and dance because they thought the enslaved African Americans would work harder if they were also given time to enjoy themselves.

The banjo was a popular instrument. Often, banjos were handmade from materials found on the plantation. A round cookie tin might form the head or sound box of the banjo, with a fence post made into its handle or finger board.

African Americans could enjoy dancing and music in the evenings or on Saturdays. If guests arrived to visit the plantation owners, the guests were invited to watch some of the dances of the slaves, such as the Pigeon Wing and the Cakewalk. For the Pigeon Wing, the dancers held their neck stiff and moved their arms and legs to resemble a pigeon or other type of bird. For the Cakewalk, several couples stepped along a straight path, turning certain times, and performing fancy steps at others. The Cakewalk was given its name because of the tradition of giving a cake to the couple who danced it the best. The Cakewalk was often danced at festivities that were held at the end of the harvest.

Make a Rhythm

Some plantation owners didn't allow much music or dancing. They were also afraid that drums would be used to send messages helping an escapee or bringing together a revolt, so they didn't allow any drums on their plantations.

Patting

When African Americans couldn't use drums, they developed special ways of making rhythm to add to their music. Sometimes they found a heavy stick and used it to hit the floor in a steady beat. They pounded out rhythms on the bottoms of pots and pans. They held pairs of spoons between their fingers and clinked them together. They used their feet to stamp out a rhythm. They learned to pat their arms, knees, thighs, backs, and the tops of their heads. Different ways of clapping their hands also added different rhythms to their songs.

Try slapping different parts of your body such as your cheeks, thighs, and backs of your hands. Can you hear how the different parts make different sounds? Without the use of drums, African Americans developed this into an art to make different musical rhythm sounds by slapping different parts of their bodies. This was called "patting."

Different ways of hand clapping also made different musical rhythm sounds. By cupping both hands and clapping them hard together, a deep, dull rhythm sound was made. By cupping one hand and hitting it with the fingers of the other hand, a higher sound was made. If an even higher-toned rhythm was needed for a song, the fingers of both hands were clapped briskly together. Try clapping your hands together in these different ways. What kinds of sounds do you hear?

Playing the Bones

Another way African Americans added rhythm to music was by "playing the bones." Rib bones were kept from a meal of barbecued or boiled ribs. Cleaned, dried, and bleached in the sun, they were held between a person's fingers to clackity clack a catchy rhythm.

Materials
Adult supervision required
2 rib bones, at least 6 inches (15 cm) long, or
   2 jumbo wooden craft sticks
Cooking pot
Supplies for washing dishes

If the rib bones haven't been cooked already, boil them in a cooking pot until the meat falls completely away from the bones. This may take a couple of hours. As they boil, keep the bones covered with water.

Let the bones cool. Wash the bones in a sink filled with water and soap, just as you wash dishes. Use a scrubber to scrape off any extra pieces of meat.

When the bones are clean, set them outside in the sun for several days. Let them get bleached by the sun and dry out completely.

To play the bones, place one bone between your index and middle fingers and the other between your middle and ring fingers as shown. Move your fingers slightly so that the bones tap together. Practice tapping the bones together to get a steady beat. Use them to help keep time when you sing "Short'nin' Bread" (see page 94).

Option: Instead of using real bones, two large wooden craft sticks can be held between your fingers to tap a rhythm.

Jingle a Tambourine

Tambourines could easily be made from scraps of metal or an old tin pie pan. Nails were used to poke holes in the center of metal bottle caps, which were then attached with wire around the edge of a pie tin.

Materials

Illustrations of African fabric designs
    on pages 90–91

Markers

2 white dinner-sized paper plates

Stapler

Hole punch

Thin ribbon

Scissors

12 jingle bells

Use markers to decorate the bottoms of the two paper plates with fabric designs from Africa. See the illustrations on pages 90 and 91 for authentic patterns. Staple the two plates together with the plate surfaces facing each other to form the tambourine. Use the hole punch to punch out 12 holes around the edge of the tambourine. Tie on a jingle bell at each hole.

To play the tambourine, shake it to jingle the bells in a rhythmic beat. You can also hold it in one hand and hit it against the palm of your other hand.

B = blue
Y = yellow
R = red

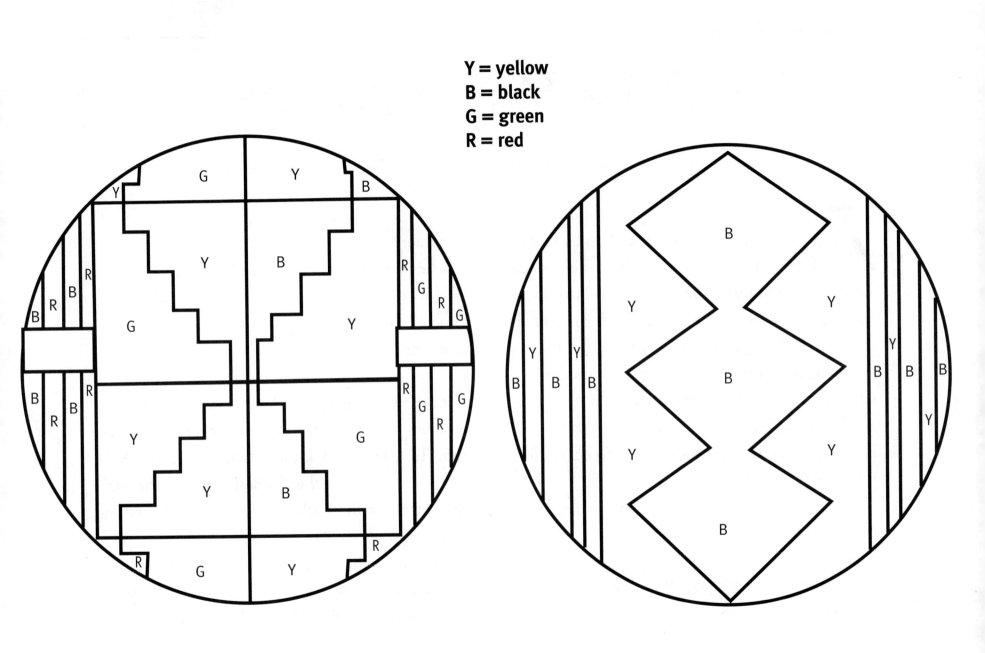

Y = yellow
B = black
G = green
R = red

Build a Washtub Bass

A metal washtub, sturdy stick, and some strong string could be used on a plantation to build a washtub bass. This added steady, strong notes to the music. This instrument was originally designed in Africa by digging a hole, pegging a tight animal skin over the hole, and attaching a strong cord to a long stick standing upright in the ground nearby. Living in America, African Americans used an ordinary object, a large metal tub for washing clothes, to build this instrument.

Materials
Adult supervision required
Metal washtub, or 10 quart (9.5 l)or
    larger metal bucket

Nail
Hammer
Plastic clothesline, about 5 feet (1.5 m) long
Saw
Broom handle or large dowel rod
Eye screw

Turn the washtub upside down. Use the hammer and nail to pound a hole in the center of the bottom. Tie a big, thick knot on one end of the plastic clothesline. Thread the clothesline down through the bottom of the bucket and out the hole, pulling it tight against the knot.

Ask an adult to use the saw to cut a notch on one end of the broom handle. Attach an eye screw at the other end of the broom handle. Fit the notch on the rim of the upside-down washtub. Have a helper tie the plastic clothesline through the eye screw at the top of the broom handle as you hold the broom handle straight up, and knot it tightly. The clothesline should be very tight.

To play the washtub bass, put one foot firmly on the bottom of the washtub. Hold the broomstick up straight. Pull on the broomstick to tighten the clothesline as you pluck the string. Pluck higher or lower on the clothesline to make different notes.

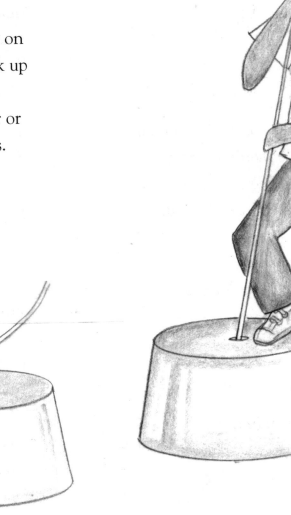

Short'nin' Bread

One song that was popular on plantations was called "Short'nin' Bread." It was a favorite one to sing, with hand motions and pantomime added along. Try singing it by adding your own hand motions and verses.

Chorus
Mama's little baby loves short'nin', short'nin',
Mama's little baby loves short'nin' bread.
Mama's little baby loves short'nin', short'nin',
Mama's little baby loves short'nin' bread.

Three little chillun, lyin' in bed,
Two was sick and the other 'most dead!
Sent for the doctor, doctor said,
"Feed those chillun on short'nin' bread."
(Chorus)

When them chillun sick in bed,
Heard that talk about short'nin' bread,
Popped up well and dance and sing,

Skippin' roun', cut the pigeon wing.
(Chorus)

So put on the skillet, slip on the led,
Mammy gwine make us some short'nin' bread,
And that ain't all our mama gwine do,
She gwine cook us some coffee, too.
(Chorus)

Alex Lomax, *The Folk Songs of North America*. New York: Doubleday & Company, Inc., 1975.

The Blue-Tail Fly

Another song heard on the plantations was "The Blue-Tail Fly." Its verses give a comical opinion about a lazy plantation owner. Use your washtub bass or tambourine to help keep time while singing this song.

Chorus
Jimmy, crack corn, and I don't care,
Jimmy, crack corn, and I don't care,

Jimmy, crack corn, and I don't care,
Old massa's gone away.

When I was young, I used to wait
On master and give him the plate,
And pass the bottle when he got dry,
And brush away the blue-tail fly.
(Chorus)

And when he'd ride in the afternoon,
I'd follow after with a hickory broom,

The pony being very shy,
When bitten by the blue-tail fly.
(Chorus)

One day when ridin' 'round the farm,
The flies so num'rous they did swarm,
One chanced to bite him on the thigh,
"The Devil take the blue-tail fly!"
(Chorus)

The pony jump, he run, he pitch,
He threw my master in the ditch,
He died and the jury wondered why,
The verdict was the blue-tail fly.
(Chorus)

We laid him under a 'simmon tree,
His epitaph was there to see,
"Beneath this stone I'm forced to lie—
Victim of a blue-tail fly."
(Chorus)

The Folk Songs of North America

Josiah Henson
(1789-1883)

Josiah Henson was born into slavery in Maryland. He was sold from master to master, and was promoted on various plantations to positions as manager and superintendent. After marrying, he escaped from slavery with his wife and small children. They traveled to Canada where they lived for many years. Henson became a Methodist minister, abolitionist, and conductor for the Underground Railroad.

In 1879, Henson published *Truth Stranger Than Fiction: An Autobiography of the Reverend Josiah Henson*. In this publication, he described the terrible conditions of slavery. He told how he often took care of one young master, following him on his horse much as the writer of "The Blue-Tail Fly" had done. He explained in detail his sad memories of being sold and separated from his family as a young child. Harriet Beecher Stowe wrote a preface for Henson's book. It is believed that Henson was the model for her book *Uncle Tom's Cabin*.

O Freedom

Often called "sorrow songs" or "slave songs," spirituals were first heard on the plantations. African Americans sang hymns introduced by Protestant missionaries or plantation owners, but they changed these hymns by adding African rhythms, choruses, and melodies. Hand-clapping and foot-stomping patterns became a part of the songs, too. The music African Americans developed became known as spirituals, a distinct contribution to the musical world.

Many spirituals were sung as a longing for freedom, such as "O Freedom!," a spiritual often sung during secret church meetings.

O freedom, O freedom,
O freedom after a while,
And before I'd be a slave, I'd be buried in my grave,
And go home to my Lord and be free.

There'll be no more moaning, no more moaning,
No more moaning after a while,
And before I'd be a slave,
I'd be buried in my grave,
And go home to my Lord and be free.

John A. Lomax and Alan Lomax, *Folk Song U.S.A.*, New York: New American Library, 1947.

Uncode a Spiritual

Other spirituals contained hidden meanings or secret messages. They were used to tell the time and place of secret church meetings or directions for escape from the plantation. Slaves would make up coded verses for spirituals and songs that explained which paths to follow to escape to freedom in the North. One song that was used a lot was called "Follow the Drinking Gourd." To the owners of the plantation, it was just another song. But to African Americans living in slavery, "Follow the Drinking Gourd" mapped out the road to freedom.

As you read through the song, try to understand what the different coded verses mean. (An explanation of the codes follows.)

Chorus
Follow the drinking gourd
Follow the drinking gourd
For the old man is a-waiting for to carry you to
*   freedom*
Follow the drinking gourd.

When the sun comes back, and the first quail calls,
Follow the drinking gourd.

For the old man is a-waiting for to carry you to
    freedom
If you follow the drinking gourd.
(Chorus)

The riverbank makes a very good road,
The dead trees will show you the way.
Left foot, peg foot, traveling on,
Follow the drinking gourd.
(Chorus)

The river ends between two hills,
Follow the drinking gourd.
There's another river on the other side,
Follow the drinking gourd.
(Chorus)

When the great big river meets the little river,
Follow the drinking gourd.
For the old man is a-waiting for to carry you to freedom
If you follow the drinking gourd.
(Chorus)

Now try to guess the meaning of these lines:

Question: What does the line "Follow the drinking gourd" mean?

Answer: The Big Dipper was the constellation of stars known as the drinking gourd. This line in the song meant to follow the North Star, one of the stars in the Big Dipper, and travel North to the free states or Canada.

Question: What does the line "For the old man is a-waiting for to carry you to freedom" mean?

Answer: This line means that the runaway slaves would eventually meet someone who was a member of the Underground Railroad, a secret society that helped African Americans find their way North to freedom.

Question: What does the line "When the sun comes back, and the first quail calls" mean?

Answer: This line means that people should plan their escape from the plantation by starting to travel during the late winter or the early spring when the sun shone more and the migrating birds had flown back to the South.

Question: What do the lines "The riverbank makes a very good road" and "The dead trees will show you the way. Left foot, peg foot, traveling on" mean?

Answer: These lines mean that there were dead trees along a riverbank on the way North that were marked with pictures of a left foot and a peg foot. These marks could be followed North to freedom.

Question: What do the lines "The river ends between two hills" and "There's another river on the other side" mean?

Answer: These lines mean that when a certain river ended, people were supposed to keep walking over the hills and then travel north along the next river they found, which was the Tennessee River.

Question: What do the lines "When the great big river meets the little river" and "For the old man is a-waiting for to carry you to freedom" mean?

Answer: These lines mean that people would come to the big, wide Ohio River after they followed the Tennessee River. By now, they would have been walking for almost a year, and it would be winter again. The Ohio River would be frozen and easy to walk across. A guide from the Underground Railroad would be waiting for them on the other side to help them finish their trip to freedom.

Escaping from slavery to head north was always an extremely dangerous thing to do. But enslaved African Americans often risked everything to try and escape. They were driven by the desire to reunite with family members who were sold to other plantation owners, by a longing to get away from slavery's hardships, and by a yearning to be free.

Nat Turner (1800-1831)

Born into slavery, Nat Turner grew up working in the cotton and tobacco fields on a plantation in Virginia. Very intelligent and deeply religious, he taught himself to read and memorized entire passages from the Bible. He became known as the "Black Prophet." He believed it was his religious duty to help free enslaved African Americans. After careful plotting and preparation, Turner set out in August 1831 to lead what became the most well-known revolt against slavery in America. He and his followers rode horses from plantation to plantation in Virginia, freeing the slaves and killing their owners. The rebellion continued for several days until hundreds of state militia and police gathered to stop it. Turner escaped, but was captured several months later and was hanged. News of the revolt spread throughout the South, inspiring thousands of other enslaved African Americans to rebel against unfair conditions in slavery. Americans living in the northern states became more aware of the harsh conditions of slavery due to Turner's revolt.

4
Free African Americans and Abolitionists

Some African Americans were free and didn't live as slaves. Often deeply religious, these African Americans believed God hated slavery. Living mostly in northern states, many of them ran successful businesses. Family life was important, as well as holidays and celebrations. Most important to them, though, was working to free other African Americans who were slaves. They often spoke out against slavery, worked hard to help African Amer-

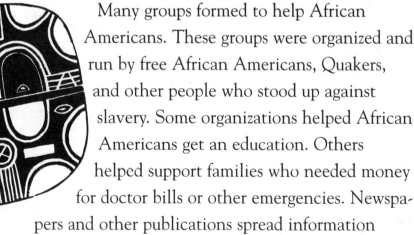

icans escape from slavery, and gave money to organizations that helped free African Americans.

Many groups formed to help African Americans. These groups were organized and run by free African Americans, Quakers, and other people who stood up against slavery. Some organizations helped African Americans get an education. Others helped support families who needed money for doctor bills or other emergencies. Newspapers and other publications spread information about African Americans, such as Frederick Dou-

Sojourner Truth
(1797-1883)

Born into slavery with the name Isabella, Sojourner Truth freed herself shortly before New York's 1828 Emancipation Act when she walked away from her master's farm. She said God gave her the name Sojourner because she was supposed to travel across the land, and the name Truth because she was supposed to tell the truth to everyone. After she got her freedom, Truth traveled and spoke out strongly about women's rights and about ending slavery. She is remembered for her famous speech, "Ain't I a Woman?"

glass's newspaper, the *North Star*, and Harriet Beecher Stowe's *Uncle Tom's Cabin*. Some of these printed articles told of the conditions of slavery on southern plantations to readers in the North who were unaware of the hardships and cruelty. Other articles advertised the times and meeting places of African American organizations and groups. It took courage to join these organizations because in many states it was against the law for African Americans to meet together.

The American Colonization Society

A new movement swept the nation beginning in the early 1800s and lasting up until the Civil War. Backed with money by the United States government, the American Colonization Society (ACS) persuaded many individuals that free blacks in America should relocate and move back to Africa. Presidents such as James Madison and James Monroe as well as other government leaders supported the ACS. Most of the members of the organization were southerners and people who supported slavery. They made plans to settle colonies of free blacks in Liberia and Sierra Leone, two countries in Africa.

Because life was very difficult for African Americans at the time, several thousand free blacks joined the movement. Many hoped that they would finally be able to live in peace and be treated as equal citizens in Africa, away from the racial tensions in the United States. Others saw this as an opportunity to spread American customs and their Christian faith along the shores of Africa. They signed up to move to Africa as missionaries.

Paul Cuffe, a wealthy sailor, shipbuilder, and merchant, joined the ACS. He was sad because of the overwhelming problems African Americans faced on a daily basis as a result of racial discrimination. A stout defender of civil rights, Cuffe had spent countless hours fighting for blacks to have the right to vote, an equal education, and equal opportunity but without much results. Cuffe personally financed a group of settlers to relocate to Africa, hoping for better business and missionary opportunities for all involved. Racial tensions grew in the United States. After taking another shipload of settlers to Africa, Cuffe got sick and died.

The reaction of most free blacks, however, was in direct opposition of the ACS. Mass meetings were held in cities throughout the North including one at Bethel Church, Richard Allen's church in Philadelphia. African Americans united as a powerful voice against the ACS, declaring that America was their home and the home of their families. They refused to allow any government program to force them to move. One of their biggest concerns was that if free blacks moved to Africa, no one would be left in America to help their brothers and sisters still suffering in the chains of slavery. Many people realized that if the ACS was successful, slavery would exist in the United States even stronger than ever before.

Black abolitionists joined white abolitionists with the common goal of persuading Americans not to support the ACS. Leaders such as Richard Allen, James Forten, Robert Purvis, William Still,

Robert Purvis
(1810-1898)

When he was just 16 years old, Robert Purvis inherited great wealth from his father, a rich, white Southern merchant. His grandmother had been a slave, but his mother was free, so Robert Purvis was born free as well. He eventually married Harriet Forten, a daughter of the wealthy Forten family from Philadelphia. Dedicated abolitionists, Robert and Harriet Purvis used their great wealth to support the antislavery cause. During the years before the Civil War, the name of Robert Purvis appeared everywhere, it seems, in connection with the fight to bring slavery to an end. He was one of the founders of the American Anti-Slavery Society, signed its constitution, and sat on its board of directors. Along with his father-in-law James Forten, he was a founding member of the Pennsylvania Anti-Slavery Society and served as its president for five years. He cofounded and led Philadelphia's Vigilance Committee, personally helping such a great number of fugitive slaves escape that he was affectionately known by many as the "Father of the Underground Railroad." He was the first African American to join the Pennsylvania Society for Promoting the Abolition of Slavery. A firm believer of integration, he supported William Lloyd Garrison's views. Robert Purvis was an instrumental voice in writing many important petitions that circulated at a state and national level championing for equal rights at the voting booth, in education, and in all areas of community life.

and Frederick Douglass spoke out frequently against the efforts of the ACS.

Whether born free, earning their freedom, or escaping from slavery, free African Americans forged ahead in America to impact their country in many positive ways. Even in the midst of their struggles to live in a society where many racial injustices existed, free African Americans along with other abolitionists committed their lives, efforts, and money to help those who were enslaved obtain the precious treasure of freedom.

Emancipation Papers

Some African Americans were born free because both parents were free. Some were born into slavery but bought their freedom by earning extra money in their spare time. Some were given their freedom as a reward or after their plantation owner died. Others escaped from slavery and lived free in the North. African Americans who were free were called *freedmen*.

To prove they were free, African Americans had to register with the state. They had to have a white person do much of their business for them, such as purchase supplies for their work, because they weren't allowed to walk into certain stores or be in certain parts of town. A white person had to testify that they were actually free, if they were questioned by the authorities. Free African Americans had to carry special documents in their pockets called emancipation (say it: ee-man-sip-PAY-shun) papers. These papers explained how a person came to be free. If they were caught in the South without these papers in their pockets, they could be kidnapped and sold into slavery. To protect these important papers from getting wet or torn, the emancipation papers were often kept inside a thin, metal case that fit easily inside a pocket.

Here's an example of the content of such papers.

Deed of Emancipation

Let all men know that I, Isaac Simons of South Carolina, for certain good reasons do from now on emancipate and set free forever a negro man named Charles who is thought to be thirty-three years old, who was entitled to his freedom when he reached the age of thirty-three years. He belonged to me from an estate transfer from Hugh Waring, who originally purchased him from William Butler.

I testify that I have written this by my own hand and I seal this paper on this twelfth day of January in the year of our Lord one thousand eight hundred and twenty-seven.

Signed, sealed, and delivered with these witnesses

Isaac Simons,
John Waring,
Elias McClellan

Fugitive Slave Laws

In 1793, the United States government passed its first Fugitive Slave Law. This made it against the law to help runaway slaves, or fugitives, escape to freedom. In 1850, Congress passed an even stronger Fugitive Slave Law requiring northern officials to help southern slave owners capture their runaway slaves, actually paying these officers for each person they caught.

Abolitionists were furious with these laws. Many people in the North risked imprisonment as well as having to pay hefty fines if they were caught helping fugitive slaves. Countless individuals as well as families opened their homes against great danger, and hid runaways from slave catchers.

In cities throughout the North, vigilance committees were formed. Their members kept on the lookout for fugitives who needed help. Many individuals donated money to purchase tickets on trains or boats heading north. People such as Robert Purvis built a secret room in their homes for fugitives to hide until it was safe enough for them to travel onward.

In Philadelphia, Robert Purvis and William Still were leaders of the city's vigilance committee. In order to help African Americans locate family members and friends who were escaping to freedom, William Still kept detailed records of the fugitives who passed through Philadelphia. Keeping these records was very dangerous because the information could have helped slave catchers find runaway slaves and could send Still to jail. However, Still continued to keep his records because he thought it was very important to write down an accurate history describing the truth about slavery. The personal accounts and detailed history of these men, women, and children escaping the horrors of slavery were gathered together into a book called *The Underground Railroad*. One of the most astonishing stories Still ever documented in his book was the time he interviewed one fugitive slave, only to discover that he was talking to his very own long-lost brother!

In Boston, Lewis Hayden became one of the leaders of the Boston Vigilance Committee. In 1851, a runaway slave named Fred "Shadrach" Wilkins was caught and taken to court to be returned South into slavery. Hayden and members of the committee stormed their way into the courtroom. They lifted Wilkins up and carried him outside into safe hands and on his way to Canada.

In Chicago, abolitionists John and Mary Jones led the crusade against the Fugitive Slave Laws. This husband and wife team were two of Chicago's most outstanding citizens. Well-to-do because of John Jones's tailoring business, black and white abolitionist leaders such as Frederick Douglass and John Brown met in their home. John Jones is perhaps best remembered for his tireless efforts to bring a successful end to Illinois's Black Codes, harsh laws limiting the civil rights of African American citizens living in the state. He was also a champion for integration in public schools as well as the right to vote.

The Black Press

During the early 1800s in the years leading up to the Civil War, many restrictions and laws made it very, very difficult for free African Americans. Whites often boycotted businesses run by blacks,

Lewis Hayden
(1815?–1889)

Escaping from slavery, Lewis Hayden first moved to Detroit, eventually settling with his family in Boston, where he became one of its leading abolitionists. Hayden and his wife Harriet opened their house in Boston as a stop along the Underground Railroad. They sheltered many fugitives in their home, including William and Ellen Craft. Hayden was a frequent speaker at antislavery meetings in Boston. A leader of the Boston Vigilance Committee, he was known to stop at nothing in order to help fugitives escape. During the Civil War, he recruited African American soldiers. He helped organize efforts to have a monument placed in Boston to honor Crispus Attucks, the first hero to die in the American Revolution.

causing many African Americans to live in near-poverty conditions. White businesses often refused to serve black customers, even throughout the North. Free blacks experienced mob violence at an alarming rate.

Through the power of the press, however, African Americans fought back. Newspapers were founded and run by African Americans featuring articles written by prominent black abolitionist leaders as well as their supporters in the white community. Pamphlets and broadsides were printed and smuggled into the deep South, where enslaved African Americans who knew their letters read them secretly aloud to their family and friends. The black press became a powerful voice, persuading many throughout the growing United States that it was time to bring slavery to an end and usher in equal rights for all people regardless of their race.

The first newspaper owned and operated by African Americans was the *Freedom's Journal* in 1827. Its founders and editors were John B. Russwurm and Samuel Cornish. In spite of great danger, it dared to print David Walker's *Appeal*, the most controversial piece of literature at that time. In his *Appeal*, Walker challenged black America, both slave and free, to use force to break the chains of slavery. Convinced that self-education and self-determination would improve the future for African Americans, Walker was committed to persuading his fellow countrymen to improve their situation once and for all. Reaction to the *Appeal* was violent. It was banned throughout the South. New laws were made forbidding blacks to learn to read in hopes that they would not read Walker's *Appeal*. A price was put on Walker's head: $1,000 dead or $10,000 alive. When Walker was found dead a year after publishing his *Appeal*, suspicions of poison circulated. Nonetheless, Walker's *Appeal* reached far and wide to influence both blacks and whites to bring an end to the institution of slavery.

Proud of his African heritage, abolitionist leader Martin Delany published the newspaper *The Mystery*. Later, he joined Frederick Douglass as coeditor

Frederick Douglass
(1817-1895)

One of the most well-known abolitionists during his lifetime, Frederick Douglass had been born into slavery and escaped when he was 21. He taught himself many things, such as how to become a persuasive public speaker and writer. He spoke about the terrible conditions of slavery and the importance of equal rights for everyone. His newspaper, the *North Star*, carried many important antislavery articles. His viewpoints and articles helped convince President Lincoln to enlist African Americans as soldiers during the Civil War. Douglass began working for the government. He served as marshal for the District of Columbia, becoming the first African American to receive a major government appointment. He later served his country by becoming minister to Haiti.

of the most famous abolitionist newspaper published by the black press, the *North Star*. This newspaper established itself as a powerful platform expressing the views of black America concerning racism, voting privileges, equal rights, equal education, and the abolition of slavery. Both Delany and Douglass spoke frequently at antislavery meetings throughout the northern states, often at the risk of their lives because of mob violence.

The *Provincial Freeman* was a newspaper published in Canada, where many African Americans fled to escape arrest because of the Fugitive Slave Law. Mary Ann Shadd Cary and Samuel Ringgold Ward cofounded and edited this newspaper. Writing about the opportunities in Canada for good farmland and integrated schools, Shadd Cary encouraged the readers of the *Provincial Freeman* to move north to Canada and a better way of life. At the outbreak of the Civil War, however, when the Fugitive Slave Law was no longer enforced, Shadd Cary moved back to the United States and helped Martin Delany recruit black troops.

Slave Narratives

One of the most effective tools in the hands of abolitionists were the books known as slave narratives. These biographies told the truth about what life was like living in slavery. Written by fugitive slaves, these books also included details of their daring escapes from slavery. Thousands and thousands of copies of slave narratives sold at antislavery meetings where former slaves often told their personal stories.

The earliest slave narrative was published by Venture Smith in 1798. Stolen from his family in Africa by slave traders, he survived the horrible trip by boat across the Atlantic Ocean and was sold as a slave in New England. After eventually purchasing his freedom and the freedom of his family, Smith published his biography.

Some of the most daring escapes from slavery were made by Henry "Box" Brown and Ellen and William Craft, who described the details in their books. Henry "Box" Brown was actually nailed inside a wooden box and mailed north. Traveling by wagon, train, and steamboat, his trip lasted for 27 hours, some of which was spent upside down on his head. Upon reaching Philadelphia, abolitionists opened the box and set him free.

Ellen and William Craft escaped together as husband and wife. Wearing a disguise, Ellen pretended to be a sick white young man traveling North. Her husband, whose skin was darker than Ellen's, pretended to assist Ellen as a slave. They traveled openly, their disguise tricking everyone along the way.

The most famous slave narrative of all was written by Frederick Douglass. It helped launch his literary career and gave him instant success as a speaker on the antislavery lecture circuit.

Giants in Literature

During the years leading up to the Civil War, African Americans had many great literary accomplishments. Because African Americans realized that history books about the United States of America were being written that did not mention important contributions blacks had made, black authors were determined that the truth about American history would not be forgotten. In 1841, James W. C. Pennington published his book, *A Textbook on the Origins and History of the Colored People*. He wrote about slavery that was in existence throughout the world before explorers reached the shores of North and South America. He explained how slavery in America was much different than slavery in other cultures, where slaves were often treated as family members and did not suffer under the harsh laws and restrictions that the state and national governments put upon African Americans.

To make certain that brave black patriots were not forgotten, William Cooper Nell published his book, *The Colored Patriots of the American Revolution*. His book includes a picture of Crispus Attucks when he was killed in the Boston Massacre, as well as detailed service records of many African American heroes. Nell visited tombstones to find key information, interviewed relatives of black soldiers, and researched newspaper accounts to gather accurate information for this outstanding book.

William Wells Brown established himself as a successful writer. He wrote *Clotel: or The President's Daughter*, the first fiction novel published in London by an African American. In his book, the main character is a woman born a slave because her mother was a slave—yet whose father was the president of the United States. Brown based this story on the information about Thomas Jefferson and his slave Sally Hemings.

Harriet E. Wilson wrote the novel *Our Nig: or, Sketches from the Life of a Free Black*. Almost forgotten until recent years, Wilson is now thought of as the inventor of the black woman's novel.

During the mid-1800s, African American women began publishing their autobiographies, describing what life was like for free black women living during this time. Jarena Lee describes the journey she took as a woman preacher in her book,

The Life and Religious Experiences of Jarena Lee. Elleanor Eldridge, a successful businesswoman, published her autobiography in 1838. In it, she describes how she managed a successful career in an age when women had few rights or privileges.

In 1845, the poet Armand Lanusse gathered a collection of 85 poems written by 17 free blacks in a book called *Les Cenelles*, or "The Holly Berries." Lanusse and his poet friends were from French Creole society in Louisiana. They traced their ancestry back to a mixture of African American and French heritage.

A poet from North Carolina, George Moses Horton became known as the Southern Bard. As a slave working on a farm near the University of North Carolina, Horton visited the campus on his days off. To earn extra money, Horton began writing poems for students to give to their sweethearts. Unable to write himself, he dictated the poetry to the students, who wrote the words down on paper. He saved his money to try to purchase his freedom, but his masters refused. As Horton became famous for his poetry, the white novelist Caroline Lee Hentz met Horton and helped him learn to write down his own poetry on paper. Local professors at the university helped Horton's collection of poetry, *The Hope of Liberty*, get published in 1829. Horton continued to write poetry, and many selections were eventually published in abolitionist newspapers. When Union troops marched through North Carolina during the Civil War, the slave poet George Moses Horton was finally set free.

Election Day

In the northern states, from about 1750 to 1850, African Americans celebrated special holidays. Free and enslaved African Americans joined together for these holidays to honor people from royal families in Africa as well as to celebrate their heritage through music, song, and dance. By the mid-1850s, though, these holidays disappeared because new laws were written outlawing them. Some of these changed into gatherings and parades to speak out against slavery.

Election Day, one of these holidays, was celebrated mostly in Connecticut, Rhode Island, and Massachusetts. In Massachusetts, Election Day started on the last Wednesday in May and lasted for five days. The people voted for a king or governor of the celebration, and after crowning the winner a special parade was held in his honor. Members of the black militia, or soldiers who fought during the Revolutionary War and at other times, drilled their troops and fired guns. Speeches were made. Root beer and special gingerbread cakes called Election Cakes were sold. It was a time of festivity and fun.

You can hold your own Election Day celebration with your friends or at school. Here are some ideas:

* Vote for a king, queen, or governor to honor
* Eat Election Cake (see page 117 for cake recipe) and drink root beer
* March in a parade similar to the ones held for many years by African Americans living in the North

Dred Scott
(1795?-1858)

Living as an enslaved African American, Dred Scott was taken from a state where slavery was allowed, and moved to a territory that was declared free. Later, Dred Scott was taken back to a state that had slavery. Believing that Dred Scott should have been given his freedom while he lived in the free territory, a group of lawyers and abolitionists helped him go to court and ask for his freedom. The court voted that Dred Scott should indeed be given his freedom. Not happy with this decision, his owners took the case to higher courts. Eventually, it reached the United States Supreme Court. The final decision was that Dred Scott would remain in slavery. In 1857 the Supreme Court ruled that African Americans were not citizens of the country and had no rights. This angered abolitionists, who then bought Dred Scott's freedom. The Supreme Court's decision caused hard feelings to develop between the people in the North, who were against slavery, and the people in the South, who supported slavery.

Parmenteering

Men who wanted to be voted king or governor of the celebration gave speeches to try to get more votes. This was commonly known as parmenteering (say it: par-men-TEER-ing). It was very similar to the parliamenteering or speech-making that took place during presidential elections for the United States. Men who were parmenteering often spoke about issues that were important to the people. Sometimes they poked fun at government leaders or well-known personalities. After the speeches were finished, a vote was taken and the king or governor was elected for Election Day.

When you celebrate Election Day, elect your own king, queen, or governor. First have candidates parmenteer or make special speeches. Then let everyone vote. The person who gets the most votes will be the king, queen, or governor of Election Day! This person can be honored during the parade and have a special seat during the celebration.

Election Day Parade

African Americans celebrated the Election Day parade by dressing up in their fanciest clothes. They wore bells around their legs and arms that jingled as they marched side-by-side in pairs along the parade route. They tied ribbons on their clothes to look happy and cheerful. As they marched, they beat out fantastic rhythms that echoed the songs they'd heard in Africa before they were brought to America. If they had drums, they played them. Many, though, weren't able to own drums because drums often weren't allowed if they were enslaved. These marchers carried pots, pans, triangles, or cow horns, skillfully beating energetic marching rhythms on instruments they'd made from common materials.

To hold your own Election Day parade, dress up in your finest and most colorful clothes. Wear bells around your ankles and wrists. Tie on colorful ribbons. March in pairs to form a parade, beating out rhythms on instruments.

Materials

Jingle bells

Elastic, ¼-inch (6 mm) wide

Scissors

Fabric ribbon of a variety of colors
 and widths

Bike horns or other small horns

Drums

Musical triangles

Pots, pans, and wooden spoons

Tie several small bells to 8-inch (20 cm) lengths of elastic. Make enough sets for everyone to wear a couple. Tie the elastic loosely to your ankles and wrists so the bells jingle as you march. Tie ribbons through your buttonholes, in your hair, and on your clothes, until you look fancy and ready to celebrate this important day. Choose an instrument and practice a special rhythm. Pair up with a partner and form one long line. March in your Election Day parade!

Election Cakes

Special round gingerbread cakes were made and sold. These cakes became so popular they were known as Election Cakes. A person could buy a piece of cake for a penny. Root beer cost two cents a glass.

You can make your own Election Cake to eat on Election Day. Serve it with ice-cold glasses of root beer.

8 servings
Adult supervision required
Ingredients

1 cup (240 g) margarine, softened

1 cup (240 ml) honey

4 egg whites

¾ cup (180 ml) hot water

1½ teaspoons (7 g) ginger

1 teaspoon (5 g) cinnamon

½ teaspoon (2.4 g) nutmeg

2½ cups (300 g) flour

1 cup (120 g) whipping cream (optional)

Utensils

Large bowl

Measuring cups

Electric mixer

Measuring spoons

8-inch round cake pan

Rubber spatula

Toothpick

Preheat the oven to 350°. In a large bowl, combine the margarine and honey with an electric mixer for 3 minutes. Add egg whites, beating on low speed for 2 minutes. While beating, slowly add water and spices. Beat well. Slowly add in flour. Beat on low for 1 minute.

Prepare the cake pan by greasing with shortening and flouring it. Pour the cake mixture into the cake pan. Bake for 35 minutes. Use a toothpick to check that it's done in the center.

Serve with a topping of whipped cream and a sprinkle of nutmeg if desired.

Pinkster Day

Celebrated throughout New York and New Jersey, Pinkster Day was most famous in Albany, New York, where hundreds and perhaps thousands of African Americans gathered on Pinkster Hill to celebrate this holiday. Originally a Dutch holiday called Pentecost that was celebrated seven weeks after Easter, Pinkster Day soon became known as an African American holiday. Free and enslaved African Americans participated in the celebrations, with some whites and Native Americans joining the crowds.

For many years Pinkster Day in Albany was led by King Charles, an enslaved African American who had been a prince when he lived in Angola, Africa. Standing with the master drummer and musicians on Pinkster Hill, dressed in his elaborate fine clothes for the special occasion, King Charles gave the signal each year for the celebration to start.

Pinkster Hill was set up like a large fairground or marketplace. There was a Royal Tent at the site where dancers performed to the tunes of banjos and fiddles, keeping rhythm with the drums. These drums were made after the African tradition from four-foot-long (1.2-meter-long) logs, about a foot (30 cm) in diameter, that were burned out at one end. The drum head was covered with a tight sheepskin.

There was a carnival area where people could buy food and drinks. Keeping the African tradition alive, the carnival booths were built from bushes and leafy branches. There were sideshows of rope dancing, wild animals in cages, and circus riding. A "clown for the day" was chosen to do special tricks and make the people laugh. Games such as egg-cracking (see page 157) and horse races were enjoyed by all.

African Americans dressed up in the finest, most beautiful outfits they owned or could borrow. Men proudly wore swords borrowed from their masters. Everyone covered their clothes with pink azalea flowers called blummies that grew wild in the area. These pink flowers were one of the reasons this holiday was called Pinkster Day.

Dress Like King Charles

Since he had once been a prince in Africa, for many years King Charles was the central figure at Pinkster Day in Albany, New York. Remembering his African heritage, he wore a special colorful outfit to celebrate the event. He dressed in a bright red jacket once belonging to a British Redcoat. Beneath his long jacket, he wore yellow buckskin clothes with blue stockings on his legs. His shoes were black with polished silver buckles. On his head he wore a tri-cornered hat. King Charles trimmed both his hat and his jacket with gold lace.

Make a Red Coat

For this special event, King Charles wore a fine, red, long-tailed coat that had once belonged to a British soldier during the Revolutionary War.

Materials

Measuring tape	Stapler
3-foot piece (92-cm) red butcher paper or gift wrap	Wide, clear tape
	Black construction paper
	Glue
Scissors	Gold lace or rickrack

Use the measuring tape to measure from your shoulders to your knees. This will be how long to make your coat. Next measure from one hip to the other to see how wide to make your coat. Cut two large matching rectangles from the red paper that measure the width and length of your coat. Fold one rectangle in half lengthwise and cut it along this fold to make the two front pieces of your coat.

Use the wide tape to tape the front pieces to the back of your coat along the side and shoulders as shown, leaving holes for your arms and neck. Strengthen these areas with staples. Fold back the front center top edges as shown.

Try on your coat for size, adjusting the staples if needed. Glue on large black paper buttons and gold lace to your coat to make it look regal for this important celebration.

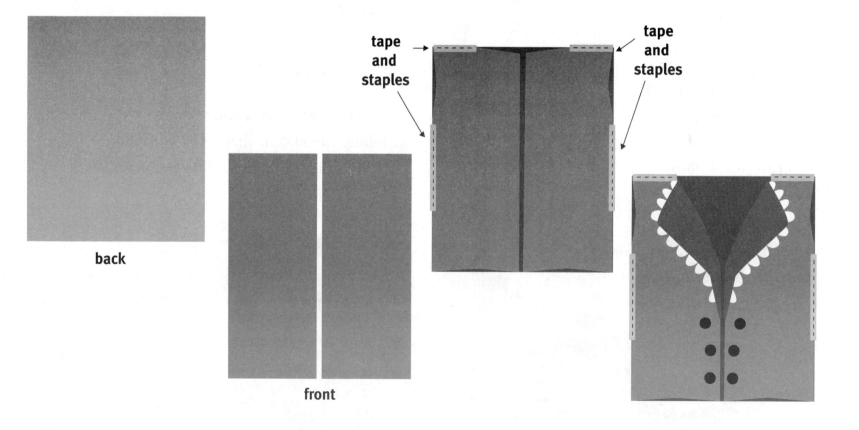

back

front

tape and staples

tape and staples

Wear a Tri-Cornered Hat

Tri-cornered hats were the style worn by men during these years. King Charles wore his with pride at the Pinkster Day festivities.

Materials

Illustration of the hat pattern
Tracing paper
Pencil
Scissors
1 11 by 18-inch (28 by 46-cm) piece
    black construction paper
Stapler
Gold fabric lace or rickrack
Glue

Use the tracing paper to trace the pattern of the hat. Cut it out. Fold the construction paper in half. Place the pattern along the fold, cutting out three pieces. Staple these pieces together at the corners as shown to form the hat, being careful to size the hat to fit your head before you add the last staple. Decorate your hat by gluing gold lace on the edges.

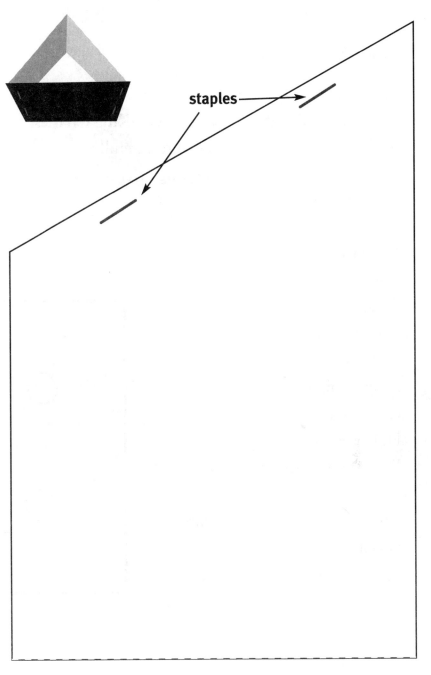

staples

place on fold

121

Make Silver Buckles

Silver buckles were a valuable possession. Not everyone could afford to wear them. King Charles made sure his silver buckles were carefully polished for this special day, shining brightly for everyone to see.

Materials

Cardboard or poster board
Ruler
Pencil or pen
Scissors
Aluminum foil
Clear tape
Hole punch
Dark-colored shoes with laces

Cut two 3-inch (8-cm) squares out of the cardboard. Cover each square with foil, folding the foil to the back. Tape the foil down on the back of each square. Use the hole punch to punch four holes as shown in the center of the buckle. To wear the buckles on your shoes, lace your shoelaces through the holes on the buckles in a criss-cross pattern, tying the laces behind the buckles.

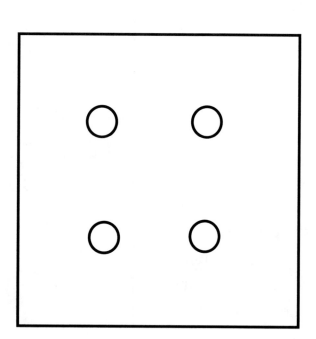

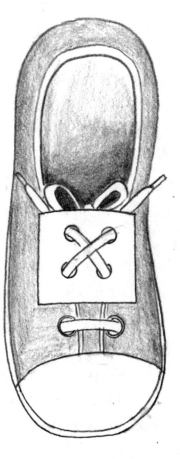

Wear a Chain of Blummies

On Pinkster Day, some people wore individual blummies, or pink azalea flowers, pinned to their clothes. Others sewed them together in chains to wear as necklaces. Decorating their fancy clothes with blummies made everyone feel cheerful and happy as they celebrated Pinkster Day together.

Materials

Ruler	Stapler
Poster board	Needle
Pencil	Thread
Scissors	Pipe cleaners
Pink tissue paper	

Use the ruler to draw a 6-inch (15-cm) square on the poster board. This will be the pattern you use to cut out 6-inch (15-cm) pieces of tissue paper. Cut this square out and place it on top of the tissue paper. Trace around it and cut the tissue paper. Do this at least four times to make one flower.

To make a paper flower, stack four squares of pink tissue paper. Fold these accordion-style and staple once across the center. Gently pull the tissue out to form a puffy flower.

Use the needle and thread to sew a necklace of blummies together. To make a single blummie, wrap a pipe cleaner around the center of an individual flower and wrap it around a buttonhole or tie it onto your belt.

staple

124

Dance on a Shingle

Dance contests were held to show each dancer's skill. One of the rules, though, was that the dancer had to do the dance entirely on a shingle, or board! All the dancers had partners who helped them. They also brought their own shingles that they felt had the best spring in the wood. Two of their partners held the shingles firmly to the ground, while their other partners provided rhythms by clapping their hands, slapping their legs, or drumming their heels. After the dancers danced, a hat was passed through the crowd to collect money for the performance.

Materials
Wide board, about 6 feet (2 m) in length
2 volunteers to hold the board

Place the board, or shingle, on the ground. Have the two volunteers hold the shingle down firmly, one at each end, being careful not to get their fingers pinched. Take turns dancing on the shingle to see who can dance the fanciest and the best. While waiting for your turn, clap your hands or stomp your feet to provide a rhythm for the dancer.

Hold a High Jump Contest

The newspapers often held accounts of the festivities each year that were held on Pinkster Day. One time, an article told how King Charles amazed everyone with his athletic abilities by jumping over a bar that was more than five feet (1.5 m) high!

Materials

Long stick, about 6 feet (2 m) long
2 volunteers to hold the stick

Have the volunteers hold the stick, one at each end. The other players line up on one side of the stick. Start the contest by holding the stick just a few inches off the ground. Everyone takes a turn jumping over the stick. Then begin another round.

For each new round, raise the stick slightly higher off the ground. Players are disqualified and out of the game if they touch the stick while they are jumping over it. The last person to jump over the stick without touching it wins the contest.

The Quakers and Other Abolitionists

The first people to speak out as a group against slavery were the Quakers, a religious group of people who believed in the importance of every individual. Benjamin Franklin was the first president of the group of Quakers who lived in Pennsylvania. Members of the Pennsylvania Abolition Society gave speeches against slavery and published articles about antislavery issues.

Many groups followed the Quakers' example and organized societies against slavery. These people often risked their lives to speak to angry crowds, or to help African Americans. Many secretly helped runaway slaves escape to safety. Others supported African Americans in court cases, raising money for lawyers, and committing their time to help win court cases in favor of African Americans.

William Lloyd Garrison published a newspaper that featured articles against slavery. Harriet Beecher Stowe wrote a book telling about the horrible conditions of the life of a slave. It was called *Uncle Tom's Cabin* and helped people in the North understand for the first time some of the serious hardships that African Americans suffered while living in slavery on plantations in the South. John Brown, a fiery leader, led violent rampages against slavery up until the time he was killed for his actions. Groups such as the Ottawa and Seminole Indians often sheltered escaped slaves.

The Underground Railroad

The Underground Railroad was a secret system of escape routes that developed to help African Americans escape from slavery. Even though its beginnings are uncertain, by the mid-1800s every person, house, church, school, store, or boat that helped escaping slaves was considered a part of the Underground Railroad.

Paths along this invisible railroad followed wooded trails, through fields, and across rivers. "Passengers" on the railroad, or escaping slaves, mostly walked to freedom. Sometimes they traveled by wagon, boat, ship, or train. During the day, they rested in cleverly built hiding places such as underground tunnels, fake closets, or secret rooms. Each hiding place was called a "station."

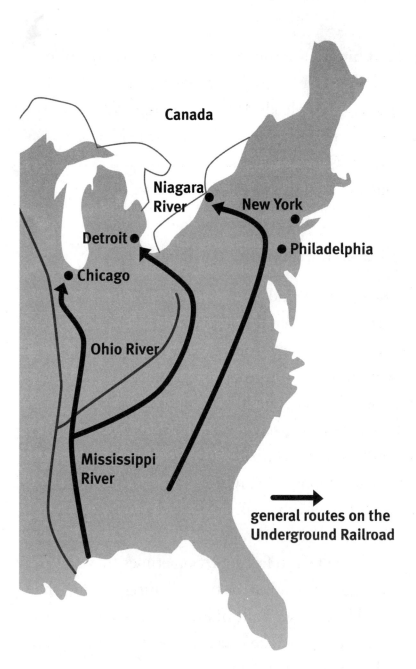

Canada

Niagara River

Detroit

Chicago

New York

Philadelphia

Ohio River

Mississippi River

→ **general routes on the Underground Railroad**

As more and more African Americans escaped on the Underground Railroad, people called "agents" established stations all along the route. Passengers would rest at one station during the day, get clothing and food, and then travel 10 or 15 miles to the next station under the cover of night. Sometimes a leader called a "conductor" helped lead slaves north to freedom. The most famous conductor of all was Harriet Tubman. Risking her life, she led hundreds of African Americans to freedom.

The Underground Railroad often led from the plantations and towns in the southern United States to the free states in the North. But even reaching the free states in the North didn't guarantee complete safety and freedom. It was against the law to help African Americans escape from slavery, so many people went into business to try to catch escaped slaves. These people were called "slave catchers." Slave catchers could make thousands of dollars by returning an African American to the place he ran away from.

Harriet Tubman
(1820-1913)

Known as Moses because she led so many African Americans into freedom, Harriet Tubman was a brave woman who risked her life to help hundreds of people escape from slavery. Once enslaved herself, she experienced more hardships and more danger than almost anyone else of her time. Traveling into the South, working under the secret cover of night, Tubman led small groups of scared, sore-footed, and tired "passengers" along the Underground Railroad to freedom in the North. She also served for the Union Army in the Civil War as a spy, a scout, and a nurse. After the war, Harriet Tubman spent the rest of her life helping the poor and supporting women's rights.

Because slave catchers worked throughout the United States, even in the free northern states, many African Americans kept traveling until they reached Canada. This country north of the United States became known as the Promised Land because it promised freedom from slavery and racial oppression.

Carry a Candle

Harriet Tubman was known to carry a homemade candle in a teacup. This candle was probably used on her many trips as a conductor on the Underground Railroad. She led her passengers at night, using her candle to help her see on dark or cloudy nights.

Tubman led more than 300 African Americans into freedom along the Underground Railroad. Even though they were often scared or suffering from the terrible journey, she never let a single person turn back and go home. If she did, she knew they might be forced to tell slave catchers her secrets or where she was. Tubman always took along a loaded rifle as she led her escapes over thousands of miles. She also carried medicine to give to crying babies that helped them sleep during especially dangerous times.

Known as General Tubman, Harriet Tubman planned every detail necessary for her successful trips into the South. She worked hard as a cook and a maid to earn enough money for each trip. Abolitionists also helped finance her trips. The money was spent to buy false papers, train tickets, medicine, food, and clothes.

Wearing different disguises, Tubman often dressed up as an old woman. When she reached the place where the African Americans she planned to help lived, she'd walk past them on the road as they worked in the fields. Singing coded spirituals, she'd tell them in the words of the song where she would meet them and when. She helped so many enslaved African Americans escape that there was a $40,000 reward for her capture.

Materials

Adult supervision required

Paraffin (available in craft stores)

Old saucepan or cooking pot

Candle wicking

Craft stick

Sturdy teacup or mug

Melt the paraffin in the old saucepan over low heat. Prepare your candle wicking by tying one end of it to a craft stick. Place this craft stick over the teacup so that a 5-inch (13-cm) length of candle wicking hangs down into the teacup.

When the paraffin is completely melted, carefully pour it into the teacup, filling it almost full. After it cools and hardens, snip off the candle wicking where it is tied to the craft stick, leaving a short end to light the candle.

Carry a Stick

Some African Americans who traveled along the Underground Railroad carried their few precious possessions wrapped in a square of cloth and tied onto one end of a sturdy stick. This stick was then carried over their shoulder as they escaped to freedom. The stick also came in handy as a walking stick or a way of protection against hunting dogs that might be tracking their scent.

Materials

Cotton fabric, about 2 to 3 feet (61 to 91 cm) square

Sturdy stick, about 2 to 3 feet (61 to 91 cm) long

A few personal items such as a sweater or mittens

Small snacks such as crackers and cheese

Place the square of fabric flat on a table. Put your personal items in the center of the fabric along with your snacks. Tie up the four corners of the fabric into a loose knot. Tie this onto one end of the stick. Carry the stick as shown.

Follow the North Star

Many times the North Star was the only help that escaping African Americans had. Poor and hungry, not quite sure where they were going but longing for the freedom they'd heard about, they escaped from the terrible hardships of slavery and followed the North Star. They knew it led north to Canada, the Promised Land, and to the free states in the North.

On a clear, starry night, take a night hike in a safe place with a grown-up and several of your friends. Carry an extra sweater and snacks all wrapped up in fabric that's tied on your stick. Take along your teacup candle. You can try to find the North Star and follow it on your hike to experience what it was like to travel along the Underground Railroad.

Once you're outside and ready for your hike, you can start looking for the North Star. The North Star is a very special star because it doesn't change places during the night or during different seasons of the year as the other stars do. When you're looking at the North Star, you're always facing north.

When you start walking while you're looking at the North Star, you're always walking north.

To find the North Star, first look for the drinking gourd, or Big Dipper. Draw an imaginary line from the bowl of the drinking gourd across the sky until you see a bright star. That bright star in the North Star.

Once you see the North Star, begin your night hike. Use the candle to help light your path if the moon gets covered by clouds. Pretend you're walking along the Underground Railroad. If you're not sure exactly where you're going, you can be certain of one thing. You're going north. And freedom is there.

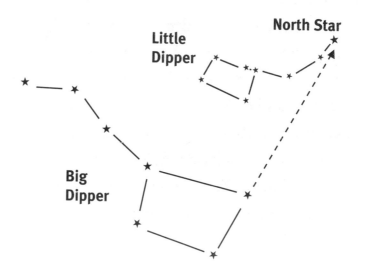

Native American Communities

A type of Underground Railroad formed that headed south into Florida. Escaped slaves traveled south and joined the Seminole tribes in Florida, hiding out in the wild marshes, huge swamps, and thick forests. Blacks and Native Americans lived together, married together, and fought together against the United States government's attempts to capture them.

Many Seminoles "acquired" slaves, but treated them as equals. The Seminoles offered a new home to runaway slaves as well as protection and survival skills in the dangerous swamps. African Americans contributed their knowledge of farming and raising livestock. Fugitives also became important helpers when the Native Americans had to deal with government issues because they could speak English and knew about the ways of the white men.

Two of these Black Seminoles became known as courageous leaders. Abraham became an advisor and interpreter, working with government officials on behalf of the Seminoles when different treaties were offered to their chiefs. John Horse was a Black Seminole chief and also helped negotiate treaties.

Two Seminole Wars were fought when U.S. troops tried to force the Seminoles to relocate and move out West. Any blacks who were found living among these tribes were sold back into slavery. It was a great tragedy when most Seminoles and their black family members were forced to leave their homes in Florida and move to the West. John Horse led a group to live in Mexico instead, where they did not have to worry about their wives or children being sold into slavery. A small group of brave Black Seminole escaped the soldiers' grasp and remained hiding in Florida, where their descendents still live in communities today.

After the Civil War, some Black Seminole were recruited to become the Seminole Negro Indian Scouts. Outstanding trackers and courageous soldiers, these men were able to survive even the most harsh wilderness conditions. Similar to the Buffalo Soldiers, their assignment was to protect and defend the new settlers in the West from attacks by Native Americans. The Seminole Negro Indian Scouts earned more medals than almost any other troop for their brave fighting. Several members were awarded with the highest honor of all, the Congressional Medal of Honor.

Along with the relocated Black Seminole, many African Americans such as James Beckwourth lived in the western wilderness area of the United States. These mountain men explored the wilderness, hunting, trapping, and fighting to survive. A large number of these African American mountain men were friends with various tribes of Native Americans throughout the West and adopted their customs, clothing, and lifestyle. Many fugitive slaves were sheltered by Native American tribes and lived with them for a number of years.

James Beckwourth
(1798-1866)

James Beckwourth was born on a plantation in Virginia. His mother was an enslaved African American and his father was the owner of the plantation. Beckwourth went to school for four years and then was apprenticed to a blacksmith for five more years. When Beckwourth grew up, he traveled west and became a blacksmith, hunter, trader, scout, and fur trapper. He discovered Beckwourth Pass in the Rocky Mountains, which became the path followed by thousands on their way to California. For more than six years, Beckwourth lived with the Crow Nation. He married the daughter of a chief. He, himself, became one of their chiefs. He hunted with them and fought with them against their enemies.

Make a Native American Apron

The members of the Crow Nation, as well as other Native Americans, often wore aprons, a form of breechclout, to cover the front and back of their leggings. You can make an apron to wear. Decorate it with symbols that might have decorated the clothes of many African Americans who were living with Native Americans, such as James Beckwourth (see page 135).

Materials

Design illustrations	Paper hole reinforcers
Brown paper grocery bag	1 yard (92 cm) ¼-inch
Scissors	(6.3-cm) wide
Markers	fabric ribbon
Hole punch	Ruler

Cut out the front and back of the brown paper grocery bag so that you have two rectangles. Carefully crumble each piece into a ball and then smooth it out again to make it appear soft like a piece of leather. Use the pattern illustrations on page 137 to decorate one side of each piece of paper. (Usually, the front piece of the apron was decorated with a different pattern than the back piece.)

In the top corners of each piece of paper, punch two holes as shown. Reinforce each hole with a paper hole reinforcer. Tie one end of an 8-inch (20-cm) length of ribbon at each hole.

To wear the apron, tie the two pieces together at your hips. Wear the apron over your jeans. Long pants were usually worn underneath to protect the person's legs from snake or insect bites.

Wear Cuffs

History books are often silent about African Americans living in the western wilderness on the Great Plains and among the Rocky Mountains. More and more records, however, are being found of the large number of African Americans who lived as mountain men or lived among the Native Americans.

The Crow and members of other Native American nations wore cuffs on their wrists during important ceremonies. You can make a set of cuffs to wear just like James Beckwourth might have worn when he was chief of the Crow Nation.

Materials

Illustration of the cuff pattern
Brown paper grocery bag
Design illustrations on
    page 137
Pencil
Scissors
Markers
Hole punch
Paper hole reinforcers
¼-inch (6.3-cm) wide
    fabric ribbon

Use this pattern to cut out two cuffs from the brown paper grocery bag. Carefully crumble each cuff into a ball, and then smooth them out again so they resemble soft leather. Draw a pattern in the center of each cuff. Punch three holes along each short edge of the cuffs. Strengthen the holes with hole reinforcers. String three 8-inch (20-cm) lengths of ribbon through one set of holes along one edge on each cuff and thread them through the other hole. Ask someone to help you tie on the cuffs just above your wrists.

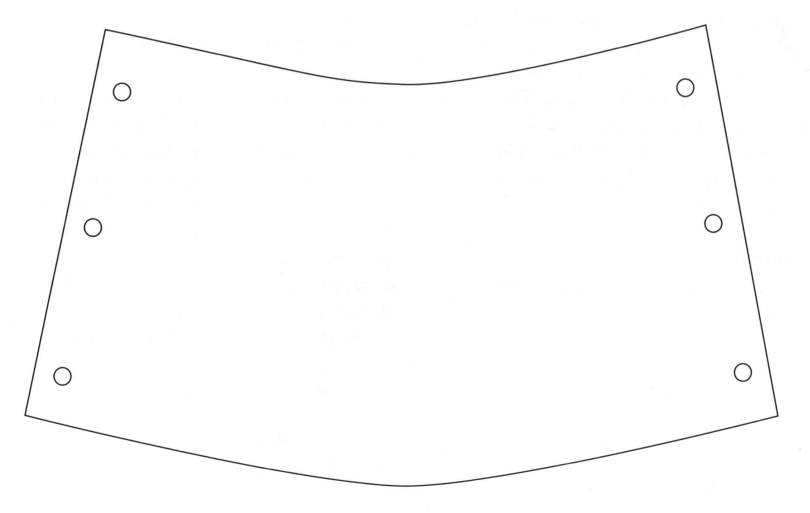

Wear Armbands

African Americans living with Native Americans probably wore armbands. Many times, these armbands were decorated with beautiful beaded patterns. The Crow Nation often sewed beads onto red fabric.

You can make an armband from red felt and decorate it with beads. Wear it on your bare upper arm or over your shirtsleeve.

Materials

1 6 by 8-inch (15 by 20-cm) piece red felt
Ruler
Pencil
Thread
Small needle that fits through the beads
Small beads, used for making Native American
    beaded crafts, about 250 to make a 2-inch (5-cm)
    pattern
Scissors
¼-inch (6.3-cm) wide fabric ribbon

In the center of the red felt, use your pencil to mark a rectangle that measures ½ inch (1 cm) by 2 inches (5 cm). Thread the needle and knot the end of the thread. Sewing up from underneath, start at the left end of the rectangle, bringing your needle up at the line on the bottom of the rectangle. String nine beads onto your thread. Now push your needle down at the line on the top of the rectangle. Bring the needle back up at the bottom of the rectangle again, just to the right of your first row of beads. Continue sewing beads in this manner until the entire rectangle is covered. Knot the end of your thread on the back side and cut it off.

Cut a narrow armband from the felt with the beaded area in the center, being careful to leave a nice edge around the beadwork so it won't rip. On each short edge of the armband, stitch a knotted 8-inch (20-cm) length of fabric ribbon. Ask someone to help you tie on the armband.

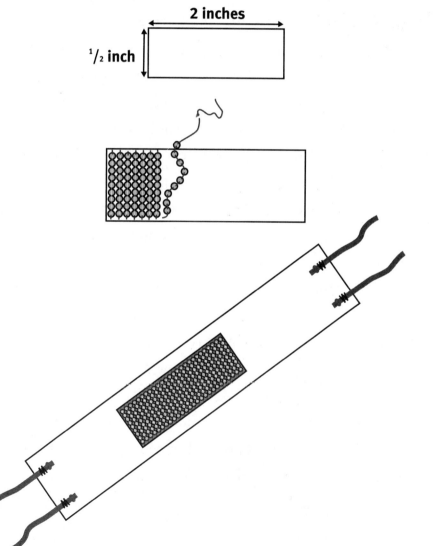

Craftsmen and Folk Artists

A rich treasury of artistic talent flourished among both free and enslaved African Americans all across the nation. Many craftsmen and folk artists learned their craft because it had been passed down over the years from the amazing artistic heritage of their African ancestors. Other slaves or free blacks were apprenticed to work in a variety of shops, learning the skills necessary to become master craftsmen in their own right. Many names are forgotten to us today, even though their skillfully wrought ironwork, woodcarving, or sewing projects still remain. However, historic records do reveal the names of some of these outstanding artisans.

Clockmaker Peter Hill crafted clocks for the families in his community of Burlington, New Jersey. Several of these beautiful antiques still stand in homes or museums today. Hill's signature can be seen on the moon dial of the white painted clock face which he made in the early 1800s.

In the mid-1800s, an expert cabinetmaker lived in the town of Milton, North Carolina. Thomas Day owned his own shop. His workshop was a busy place! Sawdust flew as he sawed boards of wood into the exact size and shape he needed for the piece of furniture he was making. A giant wheel spun round and round on his machine called a lathe (say it: lay-th). Tom Day used the lathe to carve fancy designs on wooden table legs or spindles for the back of a chair. He often had so many orders that he hardly had enough time to make all the furniture people wanted to buy. Tom Day had to hire other men to help him work at his busy shop.

His fame spread far and wide. When someone wanted a cradle for their new baby to sleep in, Tom Day made them a beautiful one out of wood. When someone needed a potty chair for their children to use, Tom Day made it out of wood. He made tables, chairs, beds, dressers, stair rails, fireplace mantels, and pews for his church. He even made coffins for people to be buried in! Tom Day had one of the most success-ful businesses in the entire state of North Carolina.

Thomas Day was born in Halifax County, Virginia, in 1801. Unlike most African Americans living in the United States at that time, Tom Day's parents were free. This meant that Tom Day was born free. After Tom Day moved to Milton in his twenties, a new law was made in North Carolina. This new law said that

no more free blacks could move into the state. For a few years, this law didn't affect Tom Day very much. But when he went back home to Virginia in 1830 and married his sweetheart Aquilla Wilson, the law became a definite problem. How could he live and work in his busy workshop in North Carolina if his new bride had to live miles away from him in Virginia?

For awhile, Tom Day considered moving back to Virginia. But when the people in Milton heard what he was thinking, they decided to do something. They didn't want such a skillful furniture maker and successful businessman to move away from their town! Who would make their beautiful beds and fancy tables? Who would hire the men in their town to work for his prosperous business?

The white townsfolk of Milton wrote a petition to the state government and asked permission for Tom Day's wife to move into North Carolina. Per-mission was granted, and the new Mrs. Day was able to join her husband. For the rest of his life, Tom Day and his family lived and worked in Milton. Tom Day's furniture pieces are still prized by collectors today. His famous workshop, the Union Tavern, is now a historic landmark.

Make a Bible Quilt

Quiltmaking has always been a part of African American life. While enslaved, African American women sewed quilts for themselves or for the plantation owners. After the Civil War ended, women continued sewing quilts. Quilts were pieced together, appliquéd, and embroidered. Crazy quilts were made of scraps of fabric sewn together. Buggy quilts were used to keep warm during a chilly ride in a horse-drawn carriage. All quilts were used for warmth on cold winter nights.

Other quilts told stories. Keeping the African tradition of storytelling alive, African American women sewed designs on quilts that told stories. After the Civil War, Bible quilts were especially popular. Even if people couldn't read the Bible, they could look at the pictures on a Bible quilt and pass on its spiritual lessons to their children. Stories about creation, Jonah and the whale, David and Goliath, the life of Jesus, and the crucifixion were popular themes.

In the late 1800s, Harriet Powers stitched beautiful quilts with the heart of a storyteller. Her two Bible quilts are on display today at museums. They show pictures of different Bible stories such as Jonah, Jacob's Ladder, and Job.

A large quilt would have four large blocks or many small blocks, each representing a different Bible story. You can make your own quilt block just like one of the quilt blocks found on a Bible quilt. After you're finished, tell its story to a friend.

Materials

Adult supervision required	Scissors
Tracing paper	¼ yard (23 cm) cotton
Ruler	fabric for the light
Pencil	background color

¼ yard (23 cm) pieces or scraps cotton fabric for appliqués

¼ yard (23 cm) cotton batting

¼ to ½ yard (23 to 46 cm) heavyweight, non-sewable fusible web (found at fabric stores)

Needle

Thread

Iron

Sewing machine (optional)

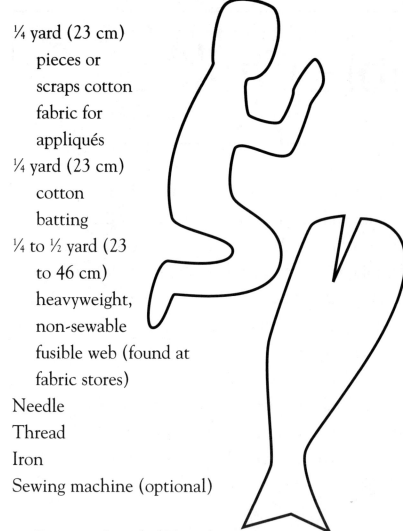

Draw an 8-inch (20-cm) square on the tracing paper and cut it out. Use the paper to draw the outline of figures such as Jonah and the whale to put on your Bible quilt block. When you have designed the outlines as you like them, cut them out of the paper. (Remember that the finished quilt block will be 7 inches [18-cm] square.)

Use the paper pattern of the 8-inch (20-cm) square to cut out two pieces of light background fabric and one piece of cotton batting. Follow the directions on the fusible web to iron the web to the wrong side of the fabric scraps that you plan on using for the Bible story appliqués. When finished, use your paper patterns on these scraps of fabric and web to cut out the figures you'll be using on your quilt block.

Arrange your figures on one piece of background fabric, staying at least 1 inch (2.5 cm) away from the edges. When everything is arranged, fuse the figures to the background fabric with the iron.

To assemble the quilt block, place the appliquéd fabric right sides together with the other piece of background fabric. Place the cotton batting on top. Use a small hand stitch to sew around three edges of the layered quilt block, using a ½-inch (1-cm) seam. Turn the block right-side out. Fold under ½ inch (1-cm) along the unfinished edge so that it lays inside the block, and hand stitch the edge closed. Press the finished quilt block with your iron so that it is flat.

Option: Instead of sewing, a Bible quilt block can be made from construction paper and glue.

5
Civil War and the Road to Freedom

President Abraham Lincoln was elected in 1860. Slave holders in the southern United States became worried that President Lincoln wouldn't support their economic interests in government issues. Therefore, the southern states decided to leave the country, or secede (say it: sih-SEED). These states formed their own country and called themselves the Confederate States of America. They elected Jefferson Davis as their own president.

President Lincoln didn't want the United States to be divided into two countries. He was willing to go to war to keep all the states together in the Union. He stationed troops in different areas of the North and South. In 1861, the first fighting broke out at Fort Sumter, South Carolina, between soldiers from the northern states in the Union Army and soldiers from the southern states in the Confederacy. The Civil War had begun.

The Union expected the war to end quickly because the North had more money, weapons, and machinery than the South. This didn't happen, though, and soon President Lincoln realized he needed more soldiers and more troops if he expected to win the war. Frederick Douglass advised President Lincoln to sign up African Americans as soldiers. President Lincoln followed this advice. In 1862, he let African Americans join the Union forces. It was decided that the troops would be called the United States Colored Troops.

As soon as the Confederacy heard that African Americans were joining the Union forces, they wrote new laws to try to keep them from joining. Usually, when prisoners were captured, they were treated with decency and put in camps to wait until the end of the war. The new Confederate laws, however, stated that African American soldiers who were captured would be treated as slaves, sold into slavery, or killed.

In spite of the danger, the response to President Lincoln's decision was immediate. Black abolitionists joined together to recruit African American troops. Frederick Douglass printed "Men of Color, to Arms!" In this announcement, he called for African Americans to enlist and fight on the behalf of freedom. Mary Ann Shadd Carey and Martin Delany used their powerful positions as newspaper editors and antislavery lecturers to persuade African Americans to join the army.

Countless African Americans wanted to join the Union Army to help fight for the end of slavery. Charles Douglass and Lewis Douglass, the two sons of Frederick Douglass (see page 109), joined. Robert Forten, the grandson of James Forten (see page 34), left Europe and came to America to fight for the freedom of others. Some men who had escaped slavery and were living free in Canada came back to sign up and fight. Other men escaped from slavery to join the Union troops.

One of the first troops to get organized was the 54th Massachusetts Volunteer Infantry Regiment. Thousands of men volunteered to join the 54th but few were permitted to join. Many abolitionist societies gave money to help support these soldiers with food, uniforms, and weapons. Their officers were abolitionists and Quakers who believed in freedom for everyone.

Martin Robison Delany
(1812-1885)

Even though his father was a slave, Delany's mother was a free black living in Charles Town, West Virginia. According to the law, children whose mothers were free were born free themselves. Delany grew up listening to tales about his proud and royal ancestors from Africa.

After leaving home, Delany attended school to study medicine, eventually becoming a student at Harvard Medical School. Proud of his African heritage, Delany encouraged other African Americans to appreciate their ancestral roots. Frederick Douglass once commented, "I thank God for making me a man, but Delany thanks Him for making him a black man." Delany and his wife Catherine named each of their children after famous black heroes such as Toussaint L'Ouverture, leader of the slave rebellion in Haiti. They opened their home as a stopping place on the Underground Railroad.

Full of energy and a gifted leader, Delany traveled tirelessly on the antislavery lecture circuit, speaking frequently at meetings across the northern United States. An active writer, Delany published the antislavery newspaper the *Mystery*, before joining Frederick Douglass as coeditor of the *North Star*. He also wrote many antislavery pamphlets, a novel, and other books.

Delany explored the northern part of the continent of Africa in hopes that African Americans could experience equal rights and true freedom if they established colonies there. When the Civil War began, however, Delany's hopes of a better life in the United States inspired him to stay in America. He met with President Lincoln and encouraged him to assign blacks as officers. As a result, Martin Delany himself was commissioned as a major in the Union Army, the highest ranking black officer in the Civil War.

Make a Congressional Medal of Honor

After they finished their military training, the soldiers in the 54th Massachusetts Volunteer Infantry Regiment marched out of their camp. A big celebration was held to honor their departure—flags waved, a band played, and people lined the streets to cheer them on. The soldiers boarded a steamer and headed to South Carolina to fight for the North in the Civil War.

One of the troop's first missions was to join other troops and try to break through the Confederate defenses of Fort Wagner at Charleston, South Carolina. The battles to take over the fort were long and fierce. Many men were wounded or died. In spite of serious injuries, Sergeant William H. Carney of the 54th continued to lead his men while fighting for Fort Wagner. For his bravery, he was later awarded the Congressional Medal of Honor. Twenty-two other African Americans were also honored with this medal for their bravery during the Civil War.

Materials

Illustration of the medal
1-inch (2.5-cm) wide fabric ribbon, striped
Scissors
Large safety pin
Glue
Poster board
Fine-tipped permanent marker

Cut a 5-inch (13-cm) length of ribbon. Fold it in half over the safety pin as shown, gluing the two halves together. Cut a circle from the poster board for the medal, decorating it with a word such as *bravery* or *honor*. Glue the medal to the bottom of the ribbon. When the medal is completely dry, pin the medal to your shirt.

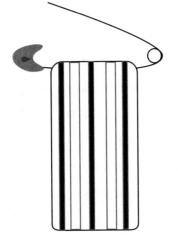

Robert Smalls
(1839-1916)

Robert Smalls was an enslaved African American living in South Carolina. He had spent much of his life working on ships. In 1862, Smalls was on the Confederate naval ship *Planter.* The Confederate officers anchored the ship and went ashore for the night to sleep in Charleston. Smalls and seven other enslaved African Americans remained on the ship. In the middle of the night, Smalls decided to steer the *Planter* through dangerous Confederate forces. He then delivered the ship with its valuable supply of weapons and guns to the Union navy. To honor this important deed, the Union made him captain of the *Planter* until the end of the war. After the war ended, Smalls joined other African Americans to serve their country and became a congressman for his state.

Make Paper Doll Replicas of the U.S. Colored Troops

Many African Americans joined the Union army and navy to help fight for freedom from slavery. Whether they had been living as freedmen or slaves, they were willing to give their lives for the freedom of others. Men fought as soldiers, built bridges to cross into enemy territory, and worked hard behind the battle lines. Boys as young as 14 joined to carry flags and play the drum or fife as troops marched into battle. Often, during dangerous battles, these young men also joined the fighting.

Women volunteered as nurses, bandaging the wounds of the injured soldiers and giving them water or warm soup. Women also did the back-breaking task of washing the soiled uniforms in attempts to keep infections and diseases away. Sojourner Truth, in spite of her age, raised money for supplies for the troops by singing and lecturing throughout the northern states. She was also a nurse, helping the wounded and the sick. Harriet Tubman served as a spy and a scout for the Union troops. In a letter, Tubman described the time she traveled with the Union soldiers across enemy lines and helped free more than 750 slaves. Leading them to safety, not a single person was lost or killed, even in the midst of great danger.

Materials

Illustrations of the paper dolls and
    their clothes
Crayons
Scissors

Photocopy the illustrations of the dolls and their clothes on pages 152 and 153. Color the outfits, cut them out, and dress the dolls to represent the different positions held during the Civil War. Pretend Susan Taylor is helping an injured soldier or pretend to march the soldiers into battle.

Susan King Taylor
(1842-1912)

Born into slavery in Georgia, Susan King Taylor was raised by her grandmother. She learned to read by attending a secret school in the kitchen of her grandmother's friend. She escaped from slavery by running away when she was 12. During the Civil War, Taylor and her husband, a soldier in the Union army, taught other soldiers to read and write. One day she met Clara Barton, the founder of the American Red Cross. After this meeting, Taylor decided to become a nurse. She bravely helped the 33rd United States Colored Troops as a nurse and laundress, traveling with them until the end of the Civil War.

drummer

fifer

soldier

152

soldier

nurse

laundress

153

Emancipation Day

January 1, 1863, was a New Year's Day etched forever in many people's hearts. On that day, President Lincoln issued the Emancipation Proclamation which freed all the slaves living in the southern states. He had been promising to sign this deed for months. In anticipation of the event, crowds gathered on New Year's Eve. As soon as Lincoln made his announcement, telegraphs wired the news to cities across the nation. At a gathering at Tremont Temple in Boston, abolitionists such as Frederick Douglass and William C. Nell rejoiced. Hymns were sung. Shouts of happiness were heard and tears of joy were shed. Slaves throughout the South were finally free.

Charlotte Forten was the granddaughter of wealthy black abolitionist James Forten from Philadelphia. In her diary she wrote about Emancipation Day. At that time, she was a teacher to freed slaves on the Sea Islands at the Port Royal district near Charlestown, South Carolina. When Union troops stormed the Sea Islands, the white plantation owners fled to the mainland, leaving thousands of slaves behind. Forten was one in a team of teachers sent to these freedmen to help provide an education. A regiment of the First South Carolina Volunteers was also formed from volunteers of freedmen from the island plantations.

In her diary, Charlotte Forten describes Emancipation Day at Port Royal as a glorious day. The Emancipation Proclamation was read aloud for all to hear, receiving great rounds of cheers. A band played patriotic music and inspiring speeches were given. The black troops marched in a grand parade as emotions ran high. Freedom! Freedom was celebrated by those who were newly freed.

Reconstruction

The Civil War ended in 1865 when the South surrendered to the North. Just a few days after the surrender, President Lincoln was shot and killed. Later that year, the Thirteenth Amendment to the United States Constitution was passed, giving freedom to every African American in the entire United States. Slavery had finally ended.

Many enslaved African Americans learned of their new freedom from Union soldiers who passed by their plantations. Upon hearing the news, they expressed great joy and jubilation. Bonfires were lit, freedom songs were sung, and people danced for joy. They were free!

A new stage in the history of America began with the end of the Civil War. This era was known as Reconstruction. It was a time for African Americans to build new lives for themselves. But many who had only known slavery all their lives didn't know what to do with their freedom. They couldn't read or write. They hadn't been allowed to think for themselves. They were suddenly free, but weren't sure what to do. How would they find work? Where would they live? What would they eat?

Many African Americans moved off the plantations where they'd lived and worked their whole lives. They packed up their families and their belongings and headed North in search of a better life. They traveled to cities and towns, looking for family members who had been sold to different owners.

Slaves were not allowed to have last names while enslaved, so freed African Americans chose new names for themselves, often picking names of well-known abolitionists like Frederick Douglass, Harriet Tubman, and Abraham Lincoln.

Conditions in the southern states were very difficult after the war. Entire cities had been burned. Crops in the fields had been destroyed. Many people were homeless. They didn't have a roof over their heads, food to eat, good water to drink, or warm clothes to wear. Smallpox and yellow fever raged through the South. The North tried to help people in the South get a new life started for themselves. Aid societies from the North sent food, clothing, and missionaries to help. The Freedmen's Bureau was established in 1865 by the federal government to help needy people and to help African Americans learn how to live free lives.

Union soldiers worked in the South for the Freedmen's Bureau. They gave out clothing and weekly food rations, which included cornmeal, flour, sugar, rice, and tea. They provided medical supplies and built more than 4,000 schools. The Freedmen's Bureau tried to help African Americans find jobs and think of themselves as employees instead of slaves.

The Freedmen's Bureau encouraged African Americans to return to plantations to work so food and crops could be grown. However, contracts were now written that explained the responsibilities of both the planters and the workers. If a planter's contract seemed unfair, the Bureau had it changed. Even though fair contracts might be written, sometimes they were not followed. The South was poor after the war and most people didn't have any money. The planters didn't have any money to pay the workers until after the crops were grown and sold. Many workers were therefore paid once a year, and their pay was often lower than what had been agreed upon.

Women joined the workers in the field. They also cooked, sewed, or washed laundry to earn extra wages. Families hunted or fished to find enough food. It was a difficult time, and people did whatever they needed to do in order to survive.

Elected Officials

In 1866 the Civil Rights Bill was passed. This gave citizenship to every African American. During the 10 years of Reconstruction, they had the same rights in every state and territory as everyone else did. African Americans began to vote and run for public office for the very first time. The presence of Union soldiers and the Freedmen's Bureau in the South insured voting rights for all. African Americans poured into voting booths to register and make their voices heard through the power of the vote.

Men such as Robert Smalls (see page 149) became involved with governmental decisions. Smalls helped register voters in his home state of South Carolina. He was elected, along with 57 ex-slaves, 19 freeborn African Americans, and 48 whites, to join a committee responsible for rewriting the South Carolina constitution. Not only was the constitution rewritten to bring more equality to African Americans, it also improved conditions for women and the poor as well. Over the next few years, Smalls and other African Americans were elected to Congress to serve as representatives or as senators from southern states. However, these hard-won freedoms were short-lived.

Hold an Egg-Cracking Party

Times were hard for everyone, so people joined together to help each other. Fundraisers were held to raise money to build new schools or churches, or to help people such as a family whose barn burned down.

Not only were fundraisers a time to raise money, but they were also a time for socializing with neighbors and having fun. At a fundraiser, the Cakewalk dance contest was often held, and the best dancer won a cake. Beautiful quilts were displayed and auctioned off for the cause. Delicious food was sold. Other contests were held and games were played.

One game that helped raise money was the egg-cracking game. Dozens of hard-boiled eggs were available in large washtubs for players to buy. Players paid a quarter for each egg they used in the game.

You can play this game today with your friends, too! All you need is a large batch of hard-boiled eggs. If you want to raise money for an event, charge a quarter for each egg used in the game, just as African Americans did during the years after the Civil War.

Materials

Large bucket or tub of hard-boiled
  eggs, enough for 3 or more for
  each player
Bowls or small toy buckets for
  players to carry their eggs

To play the game, each player chooses about three hard-boiled eggs. (If you're raising money, players will pay a quarter for each egg they choose.) The game is played with two eggs at a time, between two players.

Each of the two players holds out the small, pointed end of their hard-boiled eggs. They tap the end of their egg against the other's. One of the eggs will crack. The owner of this egg is the loser. The loser hands the cracked egg over to the person whose egg didn't crack. The cracked egg belongs to this person for the rest of the contest.

Now the players are ready to play the game again. They may choose a new partner to play with or may play against each other again if they'd like. The winner may use the same egg over and over again until it cracks. Each time the game is played, the cracked egg is handed over to the winner of that round.

The players continue to play the game as many times as they choose, collecting cracked eggs in their bowls or buckets. If all their eggs crack and are handed over to the winners during the game, players may buy more eggs to continue playing.

When the contest is over, it's fun to see who has won the most cracked eggs. The cracked eggs can be taken home and eaten plain or made into deviled eggs or egg salad. (Be careful to keep eggs refrigerated as much as possible for health reasons.)

Have a Taffy Pull

During fundraisers and other social gatherings, another favorite thing to do was hold a taffy pull. The candy was cooked in large pots until a small amount of it formed a hard ball if dropped in a bucket of cold water. Then the fun began! As soon as the candy was cool enough to handle, people buttered their hands and joined with partners to begin stretching the taffy into long, thin strips of delicious sweetness.

Ingredients
makes 1 pound (450 g) taffy
Adult supervision required
Butter
1 cup (200 g) sugar
¾ cup (180 ml) light corn syrup
⅔ cup (160 ml) water

1 tablespoon (7.5 g) cornstarch
1 teaspoon (5 g) salt
2 teaspoons (5 ml) vanilla

Utensils
Cookie sheet with
   raised edges
Heavy saucepan
Metal whisk
Candy thermometer
Kitchen scissors
Wax paper

Butter the cookie sheet and set aside. Mix all the ingredients except the vanilla in the heavy saucepan. Add 2 tablespoons (30 g) of butter to the mixture. Cook over medium heat, stirring well with the whisk, until the candy mixture comes to a boil.

Continue to cook, without stirring, until the candy thermometer reaches the "hard ball stage." Turn off the heat, add the vanilla, and stir.

Pour the candy onto the cookie sheet and allow to cool until it is easy to handle. Divide the candy among several partners with well-buttered hands. Partners should pull the taffy and stretch it between them until it is smooth and begins to stiffen.

Use the kitchen scissors to cut the strips of taffy into small pieces. Wrap each piece in wax paper.

Sharecropping

During Reconstruction, a new form of work called sharecropping developed in the South. Sharecroppers were given land from the planters. The sharecroppers also got a house, farm animals, seeds to plant, and machines and tools to use. The sharecroppers raised their own crops of cotton, tobacco, or corn. In the fall, the harvest was given to the planters, who then sold it. Some of the profit from the sale was returned to the sharecroppers.

Living as sharecroppers was very difficult. Often the planters cheated them out of their share of the profits. But for the first time in their lives, African Americans could choose not to put up with dishonest people. They could take their problem to the Freedmen's Bureau, move from plantation to plantation until they found an honest planter to work for, or move out West where living conditions seemed more promising.

The Exodusters

Reconstruction came to an end after the election of President Rutherford B. Hayes. The Democrats and Republicans argued about the election, saying the votes weren't counted correctly. Finally, a compromise was reached. The Democrats agreed that Republican Hayes could be president if all the Union soldiers were removed from southern states. This was called the Compromise of 1877.

The effects of this compromise brought an end to Reconstruction. Union soldiers were sent home and no longer worked for the Freedmen's Bureau in the South. The African Americans' right to vote was no longer protected in the South. Laws were quickly made in the South that took away many rights of the newly freed African Americans.

Violence and terror became common experiences for African Americans living in the South. To get away from these terrible problems, thousands packed their few belongings and headed West. These settlers, called Exodusters (say it: EX-oh-dust-ers), walked or traveled by train and by steamboat to reach the states of Oklahoma, Kansas, Missouri, Iowa, and Nebraska. During the Exodus of 1879, almost 20,000 African Americans arrived in Kansas—in one year alone!

Benjamin "Pap" Singleton encouraged people to leave the South and look for a better life in Kansas and other western states. He was born a slave in Tennessee and escaped along the Underground Railroad. Having experienced the taste of freedom while living in Canada, Singleton and his helpers printed flyers and posters calling people to head West. He organized transportation for many people and encouraged them to settle on western land where they could build their own homes.

In spite of armed resistance from southern planters who were afraid of losing low-paid workers, the Exodusters moved away from the South in search of a better life. Often poor and penniless, they poured into Kansas and other western states. Sometimes they became members of communities that were already there. Other times, entire all-black towns sprang up almost overnight. Even though some people didn't like their arrival, many residents collected money, food, and clothing to help the hundreds of Exodusters arriving daily in their area.

As it was for most pioneers, settling on a new homestead in the western frontier was a hard and dangerous life. Winters on the plains were bitterly cold. Crops often failed from lack of rain or hot, dry winds. Nevertheless, the Exodusters were brave and willing to work hard to make homes for themselves.

Photography, a relatively new invention, has given us pictures showing African American settlers during this time. Many pictures show families sitting in front of sod houses. These houses were commonly built by settlers on the prairie and were made completely from large, brick-shaped dirt cut out of the ground. The photographs also show how African American settlers survived as pioneers. Along with other pioneers, they raised cows for milk and pigs for meat. They drove to town in horse-drawn wagons. They planted crops for food. They built windmills to draw water up out of the ground. African Americans held an important role in helping to settle the West.

Juneteenth

President Abraham Lincoln had announced the Emancipation Proclamation on January 1, 1863. In it, all enslaved African Americans living in states rebelling against the Union were declared free. But even after the end of the Civil War in April of 1865, enslaved African Americans who lived in Texas had still not heard of their freedom. It's not known whether the plantation owners refused to free their slaves or whether troops were waiting for a final harvest to be brought in before announcing the news. However, on June 19, 1865, Major General Gordon Granger arrived in Galveston, Texas, with the official news of freedom. Standing in front of the Union Headquarters in Galveston, General Granger read aloud General Order #3, a shortened version of the Emancipation Proclamation:

The people are informed that in accordance with a proclamation from the Executive of the United States, all slaves are free. This involves an absolute equality of personal rights and rights of property, between former masters and slaves, and the connection heretofore existing between them, become that between employer and hired labor. The freed are advised to remain at their present homes, and work for wages. They are informed that they will not be allowed to collect at military posts; and that they will not be supported in idleness either there or elsewhere.

Reaction to the news included shock and instant rejoicing. People were shocked to hear they'd actually been free for over two years. But they rejoiced to discover they were now free.

In the following year, on June 19, 1866, freedmen gathered again in Texas to celebrate their freedom. African Americans have gathered every year since then to celebrate this special holiday that is now known as Juneteenth.

Because this holiday represented what the Fourth of July meant to Americans, African Americans celebrated Juneteenth much in the same way the Fourth of July was celebrated. Parades were held. Speeches were made. Games were played. Special food was served.

Two or three days before the holiday, cattle were butchered and prepared for a barbecue. Men dug 18-foot (5-m) trenches in which to cook the meat, sitting up all night on June 18 to tend the fires. Women stayed up baking and cooking special food to feed the hundreds of relatives and friends who planned to attend the holiday.

The next morning, Juneteenth officially began with a parade. Brass bands led the procession. African Americans who had once been enslaved marched next in their place of honor. Those who fought in the Union troops wore their uniforms with pride. Following close behind came people who were members of lodges or community organizations such as the African American Freemasons. They, too, wore their fully decorated uniforms. Cowboys rode their horses. Wagons decorated as historical floats drove along the parade route to remind everyone of the African Americans' journey to freedom.

After the parade, people gathered to hear the reading of the Emancipation Proclamation and General Order #3. Speeches were made and prayer services were held. Freedom Songs such as "Free at Last" and patriotic songs such as "The Star-Spangled Banner" were sung. The American flag was seen everywhere decorating floats and grandstands. People were proud to be free American citizens.

Make a Favorite Drink

Special food was made for the celebration, but one of the favorites was strawberry soda pop. For your own celebration of Juneteenth, serve strawberry soda pop. If you can't find it at the store, make pink lemonade, which tastes very similar.

Put the water into the pitcher. Squeeze the juice from the lemons and add to the pitcher of water. Mix the sugar in well with the wire whisk. Add several drops of red food coloring until the lemonade is a nice pink color. Pour the lemonade immediately into ice-filled glasses.

Ingredients

makes 4 1-cup (240 ml) servings

3 cups (720 ml) water

4 large lemons

½ cup (100 g) sugar

4 drops red food coloring

Ice cubes

Utensils

Measuring cups

Large pitcher

Citrus juicer

Wire whisk

Celebrate Juneteenth

You can celebrate Juneteenth in your school or community just like African Americans have done in Texas since 1866. You can hold one celebration on June 19 or several events lasting throughout the week. Invite everyone to attend, because the history surrounding Juneteenth is the history involving every American.

Begin with a parade celebrating the important contributions African Americans have made to our country. Make historical floats or honor African American members of your group. After the parade, read the Emancipation Proclamation and General Order #3 (on page 162). Listen to speeches celebrating freedom. After the formal services, play games just like they did in Texas so many years ago. Host a baseball game, play horseshoes, and have a potato sack race. Hold a dance contest for the Cakewalk, giving a cake as a prize. Serve barbecued beef or chicken, potato salad, watermelon, desserts, and strawberry soda pop. Celebrate freedom!

Cowboys

During the Civil War, Texas ranchers sold cattle as beef to the Confederate soldiers. After the Civil War ended, the Texas ranchers needed to sell their cattle to new buyers. Beef was in high demand in the East. Since there were no railroads in Texas, the ranchers looked for a way to herd their cattle hundreds of miles north to towns that had railroad stations. The cattle could then be loaded on the trains and shipped back East.

Texas ranchers began hiring cowboys to drive their large herds of cattle along the Chisholm Trail (say it: CHIZ-um) and other trails leading north to railroad towns. Many African Americans found jobs as cowboys, riding the trails, herding cattle, and breaking in wild horses so they could be ridden. In fact, during the time of the long Texas cattle drives from the 1870s to the 1890s, one out of every five cowboys was an African American.

Out on the trails and in the wild frontier, there was not much racial discrimination among cowboys. (Racial discrimination is when better treatment is given to one person over another because of the difference in their race or color of their skin.) White and black cowboys often roped cattle side by side, played cards together, ate meals around the same campfire, and shared the same bunkhouses.

A cowboy's clothes were very important to him and were chosen very carefully. His clothes had to last through all sorts of weather over long trail rides that took many weeks. Often, after a long trail ride, his clothes smelled so bad and were so stiff with dirt that they were burned, and the cowboy bought himself a brand-new outfit.

A cowboy wore a wide-brimmed hat that shaded his eyes from the blinding sun and shielded his head from rain. Around his neck hung a bandanna (say it: ban-DAN-uh), a square of fabric that could be pulled up over his nose to make breathing easier while riding in the dust kicked up by the cattle. A long-sleeved flannel shirt kept his arms from getting scratched by thorns or sharp branches along the trail. His vest had pockets, and his gloves were made from sturdy leather to protect his hands while he threw his rope, or lariat (say it: LARRY-it). Over his jeans he wore leather chaps to protect his

legs from rope burns or steers' horns. High leather boots protected his feet from snakebites.

Bill Pickett
(1870-1932)

Bill Pickett was one of the greatest cowboys who ever lived. Working as a ranch hand, he developed roping and riding skills. Eventually, he joined the rodeo, where he became a star performer for the 101 Ranch and Wild West Show. Pickett is best remembered for inventing a certain type of steer wrestling called bulldogging. Bulldogging is the rodeo event where a cowboy rides after a steer, jumps out of the horse's saddle to grab its horns, and then wrestles it to the ground! Pickett's rodeo bulldogging performance included biting the lip of the steer as he threw it to the ground. In 1971, he became the first African American cowboy to be admitted to Oklahoma City's Rodeo Hall of Fame.

Design a Brand

Cowboys had many important jobs to do. After the Civil War, African Americans were frequently hired in Texas as cowboys because they had learned how to ride horses and rope cattle while working as slaves.

In Texas, ranchers owned huge areas of land where they let their cattle roam freely for most of the year. They often raised Texas longhorns, a sturdy type of cattle that could survive the dangerous life on the open range. The ranchers hired cowboys to watch out for the cattle and do the jobs necessary to work a successful ranch.

Roundups were held once or twice a year. Cowboys rode their horses out from different ranches to gather up all the cattle in their area. The cowboys from the different ranches looked for the cattle that were branded with their own ranch's brand. The brand was a special mark that was put on each cow's back hip. The cowboys separated a particular ranch's cattle from the others and herded them back to a fenced-in area on their ranch.

Once all their cattle were back on their own ranch, the cowboys separated out all the new calves that had been born since the last roundup. They used their lariats to lasso (say it: LASS-so) or catch the calves. Each calf was then branded with the ranch's special brand. The cowboys branded the calves by heating up a special tool called a branding iron. Each calf was wrestled to the ground and the hot branding iron was pressed into the calf's hip. Then the calf was sent back to join its mother until it was big enough to be sold for beef.

Materials

Illustration of brands

Paper bowl, cereal size

Poster board

Pencil

Scissors

Thick string

Glue

Cardboard tube, about 3 feet (1 m)
  long, such as from gift wrap

Shallow tray

Paint

Construction paper or butcher paper

Use the paper bowl to trace a circle on the poster board and cut it out. Draw a design of your brand on the poster board circle. You can use a brand that's shown here or design one of your own. Glue string over the design to make it stand out.

Carefully cut an X in the center of the paper bowl. Stick one end of the long cardboard tube about 1 inch (2.5 cm) of the way through the X,

gluing it if needed. Glue the poster board brand to the edge of the bowl as shown to complete your brand.

To test your brand, carefully dip it in a shallow tray of paint and stamp your design on a sheet of construction paper placed on the floor.

The Lazy J   **Pig Pen**   **Rocking H**   **The Scissors**

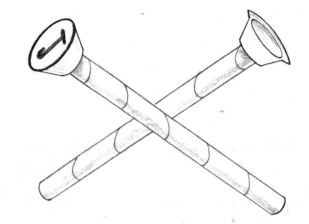

How Far Was a Trail Ride?

After the roundup, the biggest cattle were gathered together and taken on the long trail ride north from Texas to the railroad station. One of the most famous trails that was used was called the Chisholm Trail. This trail stretched all the way from San Antonio, Texas, up to Abilene, Kansas.

A typical trail crew had eight cowboys driving cattle on a trail ride. On most cattle drives, at least two of these cowboys were African Americans. The trail crew might be moving a herd, or group of several thousand cattle, stretching out more than a mile (1.6 km) along the trail. The trail boss rode at the front of the herd to lead the way. Cowboys called swing riders rode at the sides of the front of the herd, keeping the cattle headed in the right direction. Other cowboys called flank riders rode at the sides of the herd toward the back, making sure none of the cattle broke away from the herd. In the back of the herd rode the drag cowboys, bringing up the end.

It was a dusty, dirty job, and only the best cowboys went on trail rides. They drove the cattle for about 10 miles (16 km) a day, stopping each evening to eat dinner at the chuck wagon, which had traveled ahead of them to prepare the food. Dinner was usually hot coffee, bread, and pork with beans. It was served around a campfire.

Five thousand African American cowboys drove cattle along the Chisholm Trail from the 1870s to the 1890s. The age of the great cattle drives ended, however, in the late 1890s, when railroads were built across Texas. Many African Americans continued their lives as cowboys, though, roping cattle, breaking in horses, and holding roundups. There are still many African American cowboys today—such as John Reeves, who is training his son to grow up to be a sixth-generation cowboy on their 100-year-old family-owned ranch in Texas.

Use the map key to measure how long the Chisholm Trail was. How far was the trail ride? If the cowboys drove the herd 10 miles (16 km) a day along the trail, how many days did it take the cowboys to go on the trail ride from San Antonio to Abilene?

Abilene

railroad

Kansas

Indian Territory
(Oklahoma)

Chisholm Trail

Texas

San Antonio

Key | 1 inch
    | 220 miles

Bass Reeves
(1838-1910)

Known as "the invincible marshal," Bass Reeves served as a deputy U.S. marshal in the Indian Territory, one of the wildest, roughest areas of the country during the late 1800s. The Indian Territory, which later became the state of Oklahoma, was home and hideout to many feared outlaws. For 32 years, Bass Reeves brought law and order to this territory by capturing over 3,000 outlaws while using his abilities to handle a gun, dress in disguises, and speak at least five Indian languages. Judges and outlaws alike respected Bass Reeves for his honesty, bravery, and devotion to the law.

Buffalo Soldiers

After the end of the Civil War, African Americans still served as soldiers in the United States Army. Four different troops were stationed out West in dangerous and rugged terrain. Because of their bravery and commitment to their job, Native Americans named these troops the Buffalo Soldiers in honor of respect for the fierce and sacred buffalo. The African American soldiers accepted this name with pride.

The Buffalo Soldiers were stationed in the West during the late 1800s when it was a wild and dangerous place to be. Their job was to protect mail routes and stagecoach routes from raids or attacks by outlaws. They gave protection to settlers traveling across the territory. They protected workers who were building railroads. The Buffalo Soldiers were also given the task of controlling attacking Native Americans who were desperately fighting against the United States government to defend their land, their people, and their way of life.

Even though the Buffalo Soldiers performed their jobs well and often at the risk of their own lives, they didn't receive the best treatment from the United States Army. Often their equipment was old or worn out. Their horses weren't the best. In spite of all this, when they were called into duty, they fought with courage and commitment. Fourteen Buffalo Soldiers were awarded for bravery with the highest award that is given to a soldier, the Army Medal of Honor.

Jim Crow

With the end of Reconstruction, every state was allowed to make its own laws regarding the treatment of African Americans. Former plantation owners and other southerners didn't like that former slaves were given rights equal to their own after the Civil War. New state laws were quickly written that stripped away these rights from African Americans. These harmful laws were called Black Codes. Even though the Fifteenth Amendment to the United States Constitution guaranteed voting rights for African Americans, the new state laws required African Americans to pay high taxes and take unreasonable literacy tests to earn the right to vote. Most African Americans could not pay the money or pass the tests and therefore could no longer vote. Since they couldn't vote, they couldn't elect people to represent them in government. Political power in the South was now held by people who were against equal rights.

Segregation (say it: SEH-greh-GAY-tion) laws were also written. These laws were called Jim Crow laws because of a comedian and dancer named Jim Crow who dressed as an African American in his show. Jim Crow laws made it against the law for African Americans to be in the same areas as whites. These segregation laws kept people separated in schools, libraries, restaurants, hotels, hospitals, prisons, bathrooms, sidewalks, drinking fountains, and on trains or streetcars. Politicians said these laws were "separate but equal," but almost no African American school, hospital, or other public

W. E. B. Du Bois
(1868-1963)

William Edward Burghardt (W. E. B.) Du Bois fought for civil rights with a strong voice during the time of Jim Crow. He believed African Americans should be able to live with every single right given to all other American citizens. He wrote *The Souls of Black Folk* and was editor of the publication called the "Crisis." Du Bois was one of the founders of the National Association for the Advancement of Colored People (NAACP), an organization that, among other things, helped fight court battles against discrimination. He was respected throughout the world as a writer, scholar, civil rights leader, historian, and supporter of peace.

place was in as good a condition as facilities for whites.

The Tuskegee Institute

Booker T. Washington believed that it was important for African Americans to be educated so they could learn how to live under the complicated system of segregation laws known as Jim Crow. Some of his beliefs caused a lot of arguments because he would not openly support civil rights. He founded Tuskegee Institute in 1881 to train African Americans how to have a trade so they could get better jobs and improve their living conditions.

When George Washington Carver joined the staff at Tuskegee Institute, he devoted the rest of his life to agricultural research. He wanted to use common things such as peanuts to produce useful products. He became known as "The Peanut Man" because of the many products he made from the oils, proteins, and chemicals found in peanuts.

Booker T. Washington
(1856-1915)

In 1881, with hardly any money and no land or buildings, Booker T. Washington established one of the most influential schools for African Americans at that time. Tuskegee Institute became known throughout the world for its agricultural research. A well-known speaker, Washington was invited to have tea with Queen Victoria of England and invited to eat at the White House with President Theodore Roosevelt. The president asked Washington for advice on racial issues and other political policies. Washington's autobiography, *Up from Slavery*, was published in 1901 and soon became a national bestseller.

Make Peanut Butter

George Washington Carver did many experiments with peanuts and was the first to invent peanut butter. He knew peanuts had a lot of oil. When he ground up some peanuts, the oil in the peanuts made it turn smooth into a type of butter. Today we know that peanut butter tastes good in a lot of things, such as peanut butter and jelly sandwiches and peanut butter cookies.

Ingredients

Adult supervision required

Peanuts without their shells

Peanut oil

Utensils

Measuring cups

Food processor or sturdy blender

Wooden spoon

The trick to making your own peanut butter is to use a small amount of peanuts at a time in the food processor. Put ¼ (40 g) cup peanuts in the food processor. Start by grinding the peanuts at high speed for a few seconds. Turn off the motor, stir, and then grind the peanuts on low speed for about a minute. Stop to stir if needed. Continue grinding on low speed until the peanut butter is the consistency you want. Add a tablespoon of peanut oil if the butter is too thick.

Grind the remainder of your peanuts, ¼ (40 g) cup at a time, until you have enough to use in a sandwich or a tasty snack. (Note: ¼ cup makes 1 to 2 sandwiches.)

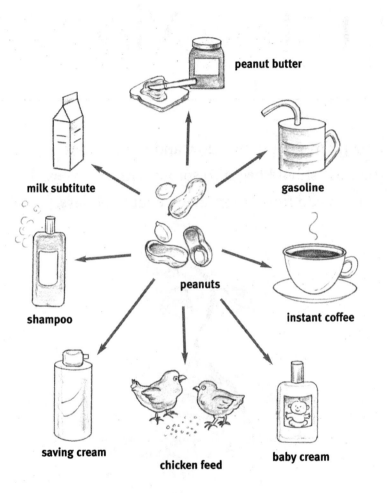

peanut butter

gasoline

milk subtitute

peanuts

instant coffee

shampoo

saving cream

chicken feed

baby cream

George Washington Carver invented many products from peanuts.

George Washington Carver (1860-1943)

Known internationally for his research in agriculture, George Washington Carver made scientific discoveries that had a profound influence on the world. In his laboratory at Tuskegee Institute, where he had been invited to join the staff, he developed more than 300 different products that could be made from peanuts and more than 100 different products that could be made from sweet potatoes. Carver's research proved that by using a system of plant rotation, farmers in the South could increase their crop production. Since cotton had been grown exclusively in many fields for more than 200 years, Carver showed farmers the importance of planting peanuts and peas on alternate years to put minerals back into the soil. As a result of his teaching, the economy in the South prospered.

Grow a Sweet Potato Vine

Carver also did a lot of research with the sweet potato. You can do your own experiment with a sweet potato by planting it in a jar of water. Watch it sprout roots and start to grow.

Materials
Toothpicks, sturdy
Sweet potato
Glass canning jar or other narrow jar
Water

Use the illustration as a guide to stick three or four toothpicks into the center of the sweet potato. Set the sweet potato in the glass jar. Add enough water to the jar to cover the end of the sweet potato. Set the jar in a sunny window and watch what happens! It should begin to sprout within a week. Be sure to add fresh water every couple of days.

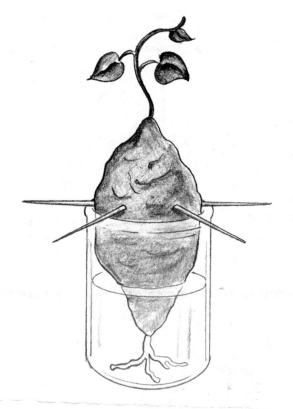

Conduct a Scientific Experiment

Georurge Washington Carver worked in a well-equipped laboratory at Tuskegee Institute, where he did many important experiments on agricultural research. He used tools such as test tubes, funnels, boilers, and jars to discover many important products made from the chemicals found in peanuts and sweet potatoes.

Here's an experiment using peanut oil and water that Carver might have done in his lab at Tuskegee Institute.

Materials

Measuring cups
Peanut oil
Funnel
2 empty water bottles
Water
Food coloring
Variety of small objects such as
    marshmallows, small plastic toys,
    bolts

Use a measuring cup to pour peanut oil into the funnel and down into a bottle you have placed below it until the bottle is at least ¼ full. Place ¼ cup (60 ml) water into the second bottle. Add several drops of red food coloring to the water. Pour this red water into the large funnel and down into the peanut oil. Observe how the oil and water mix together. Let this mixture sit awhile until it settles. What happened?

Now add a variety of small objects to the oil and water mixture. Observe what happens when you drop each of the objects in. Wait a few minutes and see if anything else happens. Let this mixture sit overnight, and in the morning observe if any changes have occurred.

Carver is just one of the many African Americans who influenced the growth of America and eventually the entire world.

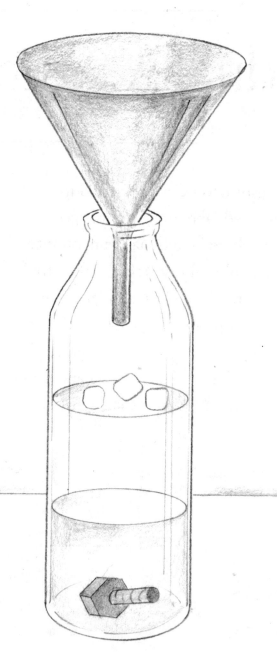

6
The Turn of the Century

Even though African Americans were now free, by the turn of the century new laws and attitudes made life very difficult, especially in the southern states. Segregation laws kept African Americans from having equal rights in many situations. Groups such as the Ku Klux Klan formed. They used violence to hurt African Americans and make them feel as if they were still living in slavery. Many African Americans were lynched, or hung, by mobs of people who were against their freedom.

Conditions got so dangerous in the South that from 1915 to 1940 the Great Migration occurred when hundreds of thousands of African Americans left their homes in the South and moved to the North. Many people traveled by train and headed to cities such as Philadelphia, New York, Boston, and Chicago. Northern cities offered hope, and the promise of safety for their families, jobs in factories, and more rights as citizens of America.

Many African Americans stayed in the South, however, in spite of all the hardships. They didn't want to leave families or friends. As the violence continued against them, newspapers became a powerful tool to make others aware of their situation. There weren't televisions during the early

1900s, so people in the rest of the United States didn't realize how terrible conditions were for African Americans in the southern states. Newspapers began carrying articles about the violence and unfair treatment. People in all parts of the country read about these issues in the newspaper and began protesting these conditions. Blacks and whites formed groups such as the NAACP to help bring equal rights to African Americans. The NAACP worked hard to spread information about the violence in the South as well as information about things that could be done to help improve the lives of African Americans.

Great Achievements

After the Civil War, African Americans accomplished many milestones and achieved outstanding accomplishments throughout the nation, in spite of great difficulties in their daily lives as a result of racism and prejudice. Some traveled to Europe and lived there for many years, able to experience a

Ida B. Wells Barnett
(1862-1931)

Ida B. Wells Barnett is remembered as the "Princess of the Press." For years she worked with various newspapers as a writer and editor, and eventually owned her own paper. Her determination to speak out against the violence used against African Americans won her the respect of many across America and throughout Europe. At the same time, this often put her in great danger. At one point, her Tennessee newspaper office was destroyed by mobs who were against equal rights for African Americans. After this happened, Barnett moved to Chicago. She married the owner of a newspaper, and together they used their newspaper as a powerful voice to help stop the violence.

measure of racial equality among their peers, furthering their education and careers. Throughout all areas of science, medicine, sports, and the creative arts, individuals rose to the top of their profession, setting the pace for all Americans to follow their excellent example.

Henry Ossawa Tanner's beautiful paintings established his reputation as an outstanding artist. A love for the creative arts drew Edmonia Lewis to make sculptures reflecting her African and Native American heritage through such works in marble as *The Old Indian Arrow Maker* and *Forever Free*, a sculpture of a husband and wife wearing broken chains that symbolized the Emancipation Proclamation.

One of the best poets in America during the late 1800s was Paul Laurence Dunbar. Charles Chesnutt worked in a variety of careers including education and law while he established himself as an award-winning writer.

At the turn of the century, Isaac Murphy became the first jockey to ever win the Kentucky Derby three times. Frank Hart was a well-known marathon walker in the 1870s. In the boxing ring, Jack (John Arthur) Johnson was the first African American heavyweight champion. In the late 1800s and early 1900s, Marshall W. "Major" Taylor was known as the fastest bicycle rider in the world. Josh Gibson played in the Negro Baseball League where he was known as the king of homerun hits.

Elizabeth "Bessie" Coleman was the first African American woman aviator. Experienced sailor, navigator, and explorer Matthew A. Henson joined Robert Peary as co-discoverers of the North Pole.

Ernest E. Just was an outstanding pioneer in cell research. As a father-daughter team, Louis T. Wright and Jane C. Wright worked together at the Cancer Research Foundation.

Important Inventions

The turn of the century was an era of great scientific achievements. New inventions were being created every day. Many African Americans joined the march of progress and designed inventions that improved everyday life in many ways. Here are some of the inventors of the time.

* Elijah McCoy invented an automatic engine lubricator that kept train and ship engines supplied with oil.
* Andrew J. Beard invented the Jenny coupler that made it safer for railroad workers to join train cars together.
* Sarah Breedlove Walker invented a hair straightening treatment that, along with other beauty products, eventually made her a millionaire.
* Frederick McKinley Jones invented the portable X-ray machine.
* A. C. Richardson invented a casket-lowering device that made it easier to bury caskets at a funeral.
* Alexander Miles invented an elevator.
* G. T. Sampson invented a clothes dryer.
* Garret A. Morgan invented a gas mask that firefighters and rescue workers could wear in emergency situations. It helped save many lives.
* G. F. Grant invented a golf tee.
* Jan Ernst Matzeliger invented a shoe-lasting machine that stitched the tops of shoes to the bottoms of shoes.

With a wide range of numerous inventions, including everything from bread crumbing machines to improvements on the electric light, African Americans made important scientific contributions.

Make Your Own Invention and Patent It

Lewis Latimer had a job in an office working with patents, or official papers protecting inventions from being stolen. Inventors paid this office to draw pictures of their new inventions so they could get a patent. Lewis Latimer was fascinated with the drawings (also known as blueprints) of the inventions and taught himself how to draw these specialized pictures, becoming a professional draftsman.

Use your imagination to make your own invention. You can invent anything! Make something useful or something silly. Make it from scraps of materials or by combining two items together, such as a battery-operated lollipop twister and an old fork to make a special fork that twirls to pick up your spaghetti noodles.

After you have designed and built your special new invention, make a patent for it much like the ones that inventors use to register their inventions. Copy the form on page 184 onto a piece of paper and fill in the important information. Be sure to draw a picture of your invention, too, just like on a real patent!

Your Patent

_____
Name

_____
Name of Invention

Number _____ **Date** _____

```
┌ ─ ─ ─ ─ ─ ─ ─ ─ ─ ─ ─ ─ ─ ┐
│                           │
│                           │
│                           │
│                           │
│                           │
│                           │
│                           │
│                           │
│                           │
└ ─ ─ ─ ─ ─ ─ ─ ─ ─ ─ ─ ─ ─ ┘
```

Picture of Invention

Witness   **Inventor**

_____   _____
_____

Lewis Howard Latimer (1848-1928)

As a highly skilled draftsman, Lewis Latimer was chosen to draw important blueprints, such as the one for Alexander Graham Bell's telephone. He began making inventions of his own. His most famous invention was a highly improved way to make carbon filaments for inside a lightbulb. Because of this invention, he was chosen to oversee the installation of electric light systems in New York, Philadelphia, London, and Canada. Eventually, Lewis Latimer became a member of an important team of scientists who worked closely with Thomas Edison called the Edison Pioneers.

The Importance of Music

Music continued to be a very important part of everyday life for African Americans. After the end of the Civil War, there were a lot of inexpensive instruments, such as bugles and drums, that had been used in military bands. Many people bought these instruments or continued to make their own.

Scott Joplin played the piano with such a unique syncopation and beat that a new form of music was born called *ragtime*. Ragtime was usually played on the piano, where the left hand played a solid rhythm, or steady beat, while the right hand played a happy melody, or tune. Known as a King of Ragtime, Joplin wrote countless songs, publishing many of them in sheet music. His song "Maple Leaf Rag" earned him instant fame. Years after his death, Joplin's song "The Entertainer" was chosen in 1973 as the theme song for the hit movie *The Sting*.

In the city of New Orleans, a new type of music developed that was called *jazz*. Jazz was a mixture of ragtime and *blues*. (The blues was a sorrowful type of music developed from the days of slavery.) Jazz bands played in the streets of New Orleans and on stages across the country.

Famous for her powerful operatic voice, Sissieretta Jones, or "Black Patti" as she was also known, amazed audiences throughout the world with her unbelievable musical talent. Performing before four presidents, and throughout Europe, South America, and the West Indies, large crowds greeted her with enthusiasm. Jones effectively combined selections of opera with popular songs to establish her outstanding career.

The haunting beauty of slave work songs, plantation hymns, and spirituals was introduced to the world by a choral group known as the Fisk Jubilee Singers. In an effort to raise money for Fisk University, this group toured in the 1870s throughout the United States and Europe, performing in front of such notables as President Grant as well as Queen Victoria in England. Not only did they raise enough money to help their floundering school, their efforts memorialized important songs rooted in the heritage of African Americans, which might have otherwise been lost forever.

Harlem Renaissance

By the 1920s, there were so many talented African American musicians, so many new styles of music being played, and so many new artists and writers, that this era was known as the Harlem Renaissance (say it: REN-uh-sahnts). The reason this period of time became known as the Harlem Renaissance was that *renaissance* means "rebirth," and Harlem was the main place this rebirth of culture took place.

Harlem is a section of New York City where African American musicians, writers, artists, and performers gathered to express their thoughts and feelings about being black in America. Articles and books were published. Paintings were displayed and sold. Musicians and performers made records and entertained large crowds of people. Because of the enthusiasm and success of the Harlem Renaissance, African Americans everywhere were encouraged to take pride in who they were by expressing their feelings through art, literature, and music.

An outstanding student, Alain Leroy Locke graduated with honors from Harvard University. He

Langston Hughes
(1902-1967)

Skilled in all types of writing, Langston Hughes is remembered best as the "Poet Laureate of Harlem." A poet laureate (say it: LOR-ee-et) is someone who is the best poetry writer. It is generally accepted that Hughes was the best poetry writer during the Harlem Renaissance. As a teenager, Hughes left his Mississippi home to travel the world and write. He wrote poetry about the experience of being African American using a musically rhythmic style. Best known for his poetry, Hughes also wrote children's books, novels, plays, and song lyrics. He won many important awards for his work.

also became the first African American Rhodes scholar. His classic, *The New Negro*, contained examples pulsing from the heartbeat of the Harlem Renaissance with essays, poetry, and stories by such literary giants as Langston Hughes, Countee Cullen, and Jean Toomer.

As a writer, Claude McKay opened a window for the world to see what life was like for African Americans. Truly gifted, he used his talents to write with passion and bare honesty, in a way no one had ever quite written before. Zora Neale Hurston had a heart for folklore and an ear for people's conversations. Her writing is rich in dialect and filled with tradition. She conducted research by traveling throughout the South and the Caribbean to collect African American folktales.

Horace Pippin's paintings were remarkable partly because he was a self-taught artist. His work was highly personal and showed scenes from his memory, such as in the painting *Domino Players*. After his shoulder was injured in World War I, Pippin burned pictures onto wood. Not only was this

Augusta Savage
(1900-1962)

As a sculptor, Augusta Savage brought many African American heroes to life by sculpting their likenesses. Even as a young child, she loved to shape things out of clay. Her joy of art continued as she pursued formal training in the United States as well as Paris. Her bust of W. E. B. Du Bois established her success. With a vision for helping other African American artists, Savage opened an art school in Harlem where she taught such future artists as Jacob Lawrence. She also was the supervisor of government art projects in Harlem and New York City. Her sculpture portraying the important contributions of African Americans to the world of music, *Lift Every Voice and Sing*, is one of her most famous works.

187

therapeutic method helpful to strengthen his arm, but he created pictures of scenes from the war to help work through his troubled memories of being a soldier in France. His paintings are prized by museums and art collectors today.

James VanDerZee and Oscar Micheaux used a new art form to achieve their success. A photographer, VanDerZee captured the Harlem Renaissance in pictures. He took photographs of famous African Americans as well as scenes from common, everyday life in Harlem. Through his many photographs, he documented important events and organizations such as parades, dance classes, and sports teams. His amazing career spanned across the decades to include such modern-day African American personalities as Bill Cosby.

Oscar Micheaux was a filmmaker. As writer, director, and producer, he focused mostly on making movies for African American audiences. At a time when Hollywood was not open to producing movies starring African American actors or themes, Micheaux was a pioneer.

African American musicians set the stage and influenced music all across America. Outstanding talent was displayed by such greats as W. C. Handy, Jelly Roll Morton, and Fletcher Henderson. Working between New Orleans, Chicago, and New York City, these legendary giants set America's feet tapping and filled dance halls with energetic crowds.

Bessie Smith
(1894-1937)

Bessie Smith was called the "Empress of the Blues" because of her deep, beautiful voice. She earned the highest salary of any African American performer at that time. She recorded more than 160 songs and her records sold very quickly. Smith's singing career began in small theaters and local stages, but soon she was a star with her own group of traveling musicians.

When Duke Ellington hit the scene in the late 1920s, he was quickly booked with his orchestra at the famous Cotton Club in New York City. He recorded many popular songs during the Harlem Renaissance and on through the decades to become one of America's most-loved composers and talented bandleaders.

In the arena of classical music, William Grant Still was famous as a composer of music for symphonies, operas, and ballets. His style combined a study of classical form with melodies and rhythm from jazz and blues to create a unique sound. He achieved many firsts as a musician including being the first African American to have a symphony performed by a major orchestra.

Marian Anderson's rich voice filled her listeners with awe. The first African American to perform in a major role with the Metropolitan Opera Company, she traveled a long, hard road against prejudice and racism during her amazing musical career. In 1939, the Daughters of the American Revolution refused to allow her to sing at Constitution Hall in Washington, D.C., because of her race. The news spread like wildfire. Public indignation was so strong at this outrage that Anderson was invited to sing at the Lincoln Memorial instead. A true hero, Marian Anderson became a symbol of triumph and pride.

Louis Armstrong
(1898-1971)

Louis Armstrong played the cornet, a trumpet, with such imagination and skill that he became known as one of the world's best musicians. Affectionately known as "Satchmo," Armstrong began his career playing in the Creole Jazz Band in Chicago. Soon he not only played his instrument, but he also sang and led bands. Everywhere he went, his imaginative style of playing the cornet and the way he used his voice made him a favorite. He performed to audiences throughout the world. Many of his songs were recorded on records.

Play the Cornet

A cornet is an instrument that looks and sounds like the trumpet. The difference between a cornet and a trumpet is that a cornet has a longer tube and a deeper mouthpiece than a trumpet. Louis Armstrong was famous for playing songs on his cornet in new and different ways. He would slow some parts of a song down and play other parts very fast. He would add new notes that went along with the different notes in the song. By using his imagination, he made old songs sound brand-new.

You can make a cornet to play, too. Try playing a favorite song of yours, but pretend you're Louis Armstrong by trying to play the song in a different way than it's ever been played before.

Materials

3-foot (1 m) length of clear vinyl tubing, measuring ½ inch (1 cm) inside the tube (available in the plumbing department at hardware stores)

Clear tape

Medium-sized funnel with the opening on the spout measuring less than ½ inch (1 cm)

Roll up the tube to form the body of the cornet, using the illustration as a guide. To hold its shape, wrap tape around the part that overlaps. Place the funnel in one end, taping if necessary. Hum a song into the other end of the tubing to play your cornet.

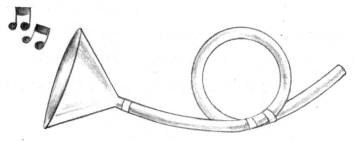

The World at War . . . Twice

The United States entered World War I in 1917. "Make the World Safe for Democracy" was the cry that echoed throughout America. This cry affected African Americans deeply, because they wanted to experience freedom and democracy throughout the world and in their own personal lives as well.

Many African Americans volunteered to serve in the military. Often, they were not allowed to join because of racial discrimination. Those who were able to join were often treated unequally in many unfair ways. They weren't given the positions they were qualified to hold. Many times, they had to cook or clean instead of fight.

In spite of the hardships, African Americans who were able to join the war effort won honor and recognition on the battlefields. In Europe, African Americans were treated with more respect and honor than at home.

World War I became a turning point for African Americans. The soldiers who traveled to Europe found out what it was like to be treated as equals.

African Americans who didn't join the military were able to get better jobs in factories producing weapons and supplies for the war. The hope of freedom, democracy, and a better life became goals that seemed possible.

"Harlem's Own" was the proud name of the troop that won more medals than any other American fighting unit. The 369th Regiment, an all-black unit, won worldwide fame and respect. One time, two of its soldiers protected American forces from German attack by hand-to-hand combat. When Henry Johnson and Needham Roberts were on guard duty on the front lines with the 369th in France, they heard wire cutters snipping wires and realized they were under attack. In spite of serious wounds, they held their positions by throwing grenades and stopping each German soldier who advanced. Both men were awarded the French Croix de Guerre for their amazing courage and skill.

The 369th was also famous for its military band, led by the already well-known bandleader Lieutenant James Reese Europe. The band traveled throughout Europe, entertaining soldiers, war leaders, and social dignitaries alike with enthusiastic performances of the new American style of music, featuring great jazz sessions that made every listener's feet itch to dance.

Japan attacked the United States at Pearl Harbor, Hawaii, in 1941, plunging America into World War II. Dorie Miller was on board the battleship *Arizona* when Japan attacked. Running to a machine gun, Miller's expert shooting brought down four enemy planes. An instant hero, Miller was awarded the Navy Cross for his brave action in the midst of battle.

People everywhere were committed to joining the effort to win the war. Hundreds of thousands of African Americans joined the military to fight for their country. Those at home did everything they could to help, including working in factories to make supplies for the war.

Benjamin Davis Sr. faced discrimination throughout his lengthy military career, yet rose up to become the first African American general in the United States Army. Serving through both World Wars, Davis Sr. also taught various military classes to African American troops. A strong sup-porter of equal rights within the military, he was appointed head of race relations.

His son, Benjamin Davis Jr., graduated near the top of his class from West Point. A gifted leader, he became the commander of the first class of Tuskegee Airmen. He also joined his father in the fight to end military segregation. Davis Jr. rose up through the ranks to become the first African American general of the United States Air Force.

Davis Jr. and the Tuskegee Airmen trained at the famous Tuskegee Institute in Alabama. Almost 1,000 men trained as pilots. One thousand more trained as airplane support teams. Four fighter squadrons were formed that fought during World War II, flying mostly over Italy. Their outstanding record amazed people throughout the world. When the Tuskegee Airmen escorted bombers into Europe, they didn't lose a single bomber. Their fighter pilots shot down and destroyed numerous enemy planes, including a German warship. By the end of the war, these heroic men were awarded 100 Distinguished Flying Crosses.

While the country was at war fighting for democracy, the NAACP became a stronger voice as it tried to fight the war against racial prejudice in the military and in all areas of life throughout America. The NAACP took many cases to court, and some of these cases went all the way to the United States Supreme Court. Many important cases were won in favor of equal rights for African Americans.

Creative Milestones

Even though the Great Depression and two world wars brought an end to the Harlem Renaissance, African Americans continued to achieve significant milestones in the creative arts. Rock and roll rocked the nation with the sensational twang of Chuck Berry's electric guitar. Teens across America fell in love with songs like "Maybellene," "Roll Over Beethoven," and "Johnny B. Goode." Performing to cheering audiences, Chuck Berry danced his way across the stage with his famous "duck walk." Berry's definitive style influenced such musical groups as the Beatles and the Beach Boys.

Dancers Katherine Dunham and Pearl Primus amazed audiences with their energetic ability and

Charles Richard Drew (1904-1950)

A physician, Charles Drew is best known for his work with blood. An outstanding athlete and highly educated scholar, Charles Drew's interest in medicine led him to research blood. He discovered a way to store blood and established the first successful blood bank. During World War II, England asked him to create blood banks for soldiers. He also did the same for the American Red Cross. Because of his work, many thousands of soldiers' lives were saved. He received countless awards for his work, with many schools and medical buildings being named after this important man.

unique choreography. Their careers paralleled each other in several ways. Both studied the influences of African dance. Both interpreted their cultural roots into new expressions of dance and movement.

Both also believed in the importance of education, teaching the next generation to express themselves through the beauty and creative form of dance. Both received numerous awards and reached international fame.

In theater and film, Lorraine Hansberry's award-winning play *A Raisin in the Sun* became a movie starring Sidney Poitier. Hansberry achieved many firsts in her career as author and playwright, cut short by her death from cancer. Poitier went on to become a famous movie star, cast in many roles that for the first time portrayed a black man interacting with whites in mainstream films as an intelligent individual, with complex feelings of his own, worthy of respect.

Growing up in Harlem, artist Jacob Lawrence was influenced by such greats as sculptor Augusta Savage. He painted many subjects, such as Frederick Douglass and Harriet Tubman, in a series of paintings. His interpretation of African American history in his paintings established Lawrence as one of the best artists in America. He used bold colors and simple forms to energize his paintings that por-

Mary McLeod Bethune (1875-1955)

From the South Carolina cotton fields, Mary McLeod Bethune rose up with dedication and courage to become an outstanding educator and an advisor to four presidents. As a teen, she longed to be a missionary to Africa, but after graduating from Bible college was turned down as a missionary because of her young age. She moved to Florida, where she established a small school for young black women that eventually became a very important college, Bethune-Cookman College. Supporting educational causes, Bethune also became involved with the government. She served as a member of President Franklin Delano Roosevelt's "Black Cabinet," giving him advice about racial issues in America.

trayed the struggles and triumphs of blacks living in America.

In literature, African American writers earned many awards and honors, including the coveted Pulitzer Prize, awarded to Gwendolyn Brooks, the first African American poet to win this prestigious award. Richard Wright's popular book *Native Son*, Ralph Ellison's classic *Invisible Man*, and James Baldwin's first novel *Go Tell It on the Mountain* established black authors as strong voices in the hearts and minds of American readers.

Sports, America's Favorite Games

Many African Americans were encouraged by successful sports personalities. Before going on to establish a successful acting career, Paul Robeson was a star player on the football field. Jesse Owens won four gold medals at the 1936 Olympics in the track-and-field events. Joe Louis won the heavyweight title for boxing in 1937. For more than a decade, John Davis held Olympic and world championship titles in weightlifting. Alice Coachman

Davis won a gold medal in track and field in the 1948 Olympics. The Rens and the Harlem Globetrotters were all-black teams whose players dominated the basketball floor with their skill and scoring ability.

Jackie Robinson joined the Brooklyn Dodgers in 1947, becoming the first African American to play baseball in the segregated major leagues. Robinson's skill on the baseball field and his character and commitment to help get rid of racial discrimination became the standard to live up to for many African Americans.

Robinson opened the doors for such baseball greats as Satchel Paige and Willie Mays to play major league baseball on integrated teams. Satchel Paige's legendary pitching kept fans on the edge of their seats. To the roar of the cheering crowds, Willie Mays stacked up high numbers throughout his baseball career in home runs and stolen bases.

America struggled with racism and segregation laws. Yet in the midst of hardship, sports figures played with a passion as representatives of equality and pride for every American.

Track-and-Field Day

Jesse Owens was the star of track-and-field sports events. He began by setting school records for racing and jumping. When he went to Ohio State University, he joined the track team. As a member of that team, Owens had one of the best days of his life in 1935. That day is also remembered as the most important day in the history of track-and-field events. Within 45 minutes, Owens set three world records and tied a fourth world record! He was one of the best runners in the world.

To honor the memory of Owens, you can hold a Track-and-Field Day with your friends. Run the 100-meter dash. Hold a 400-meter relay. See who can jump the farthest on the long jump. Be sure to give the winners medals to wear!

100-Meter Race

Jesse Owens went to the Olympics in 1936. Even though it was held in Germany during the dangerous time when Adolf Hitler was the country's leader, Jesse Owens was determined to do his best. For the 100-meter race, Jesse Owens tied the Olympic record. He ran that race in just 10.3 seconds. Jesse Owens also ran the 200-meter race, where he set a new world record for his speed. He ran the 200-meter race in only 20.7 seconds!

Materials

Large playing field
1 ball of string
Meter stick
Long rope
Long ribbon

To hold a 100-meter race, measure off a straight area on the field that is 100 meters in length. To measure the field, first cut a piece of string that measures 10 meters long. (If you don't have a meter stick, 39.37 inches is equivalent to one meter.) Place the 10-meter string on the ground end-to-end for a total of 10 times to find the 100-meter length. Make a starting line at one end by laying the rope across the field. Line up the runners side by side behind the rope. At the other end, have two volunteers hold a long ribbon across the field to make the finish line.

At a signal, race in a straight line toward the finish line. The first runner to touch the ribbon wins the race.

400-Meter Relay

In the 1936 Olympics, Jesse Owens was part of the American relay team. A relay race is when a team of runners each run a short part of the race. If they all run their parts faster than the other teams, together their team can win the race. Jesse Owens and his team set a new Olympic record for the 400-meter relay that year.

Materials

Four players for each team
Oval-shaped track area
Metric field-measuring device
Cardboard paper towel tube, one per team

Measure an area of the track that is 400 meters long. (If you don't have a track, arrange cones

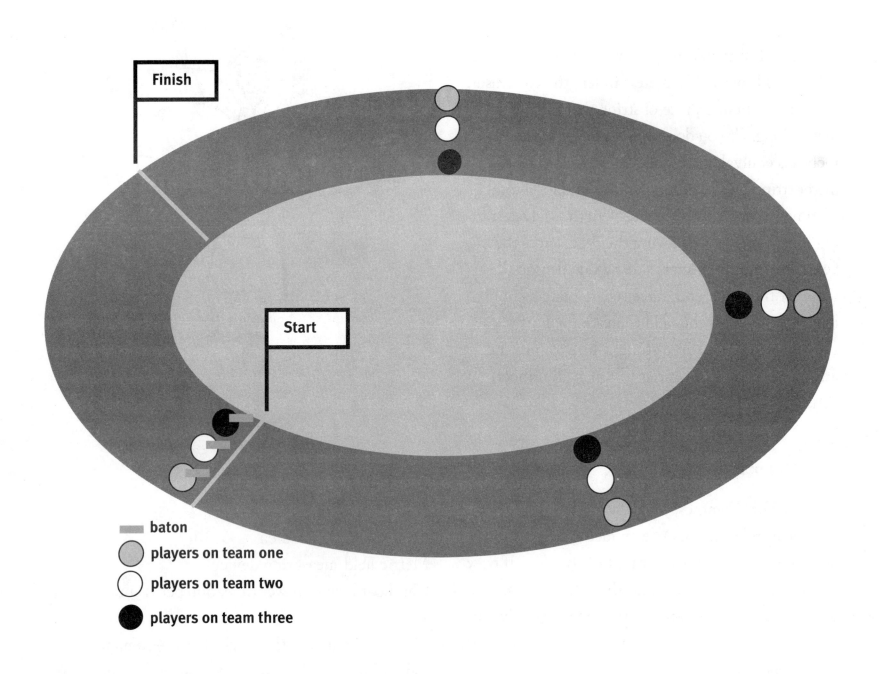

baton

players on team one

players on team two

players on team three

around a field to form one.) Station the four players of each team along the oval track, spacing them evenly apart. One player from each team should stand at the starting line.

The runners at the starting line should each hold their baton (say it: bah-TAHN), or cardboard tube. At the signal to start the race, these runners race along the track until they come up to the second member on their team. As soon as the first runner hands the second runner the baton, the second runner takes off. The second runner hands the baton to the third runner. The third runner hands the baton to the fourth runner on the team. The fourth runner races down the track and carries the baton across the finish line. The first team to cross the finish line wins the race.

The Long Jump

When Jesse Owens jumped in the long jump for the 1936 Olympics, it seemed like he was flying. One reporter wrote that it looked as if he might jump the whole way out of Germany! He set an Olympic record by jumping 8.06 meters!

Materials

Small, level area of field
Rope
Markers
Meter stick

On a small, level area of the field, place a rope on the ground as the starting point for the long jump. One at a time, run up toward the rope. When you reach the rope, jump as far forward as you can. Mark where each player lands and measure the distance. Set a marker at 8.06 meters to compare your jumps to Owens's jump.

Win a Medal

Jesse Owens won four gold medals at the 1936 Olympics in Germany. When you hold your track-and-field day, you can give medals to the winners, too! Give gold medals to the first place winners, silver medals to the second place winners, and bronze medals to the third place winners just like in the Olympics.

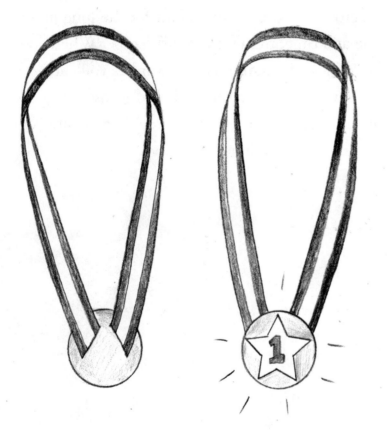

Materials

Adult supervision required

Metal lids (with rounded edges) from frozen juice containers

Gold, silver, and bronze metallic paint

½-inch (1-cm) wide-fabric ribbon with red, white, and blue stripes

Scissors

Hot glue gun or craft glue

Decorate the metal lids with the gold, silver, and bronze paint for first, second, and third place. Cut the ribbon into 3 15-inch (38-cm) pieces. Glue both ends of one ribbon to the back of each decorated metal lid to form the medal. After each event is held on your track-and-field day, present the winners with their medals, just like the Olympic medals were presented to Owens.

7
The Civil Rights Movement

African Americans lived in a country where lessons about democracy were taught in every school. In a democracy, every person was supposed to be equally as important as everyone else. The United States Constitution clearly stated that these democratic ideas were the law in America.

Yet throughout many parts of the United States, African Americans were not being treated in a way that obeyed the Constitution. For instance, black children were not allowed to go to schools where white children went. Black people couldn't eat at the same table in a restaurant where white people were eating.

And even while they were being forced to ride only in the back of a bus, African Americans were also required to give up their seats on the bus if all the seats were full and a white person got on.

By the 1950s, many African Americans decided that it was time to experience democracy for themselves as Americans. They knew it was time to get rid of segregation laws and other laws against equality. African Americans decided it was time to work together for civil rights, or the personal rights every American was supposed to have. This joining together of African Americans and others who believed in equal rights for all people was called the Civil Rights Movement.

The Civil Rights Movement was a time for African Americans to bring changes to America, and many chose to do this by using nonviolence. Led by such leaders as Dr. Martin Luther King Jr., the Civil Rights Movement affected people in America like no other movement had ever done before.

How One Woman Made a Difference

A major event that brought attention to the Civil Rights Movement began with an ordinary person named Rosa Parks, who did an extraordinary thing in Montgomery, Alabama. Rosa Parks was a seamstress. On December 1, 1955, she felt tired from her long day at work. The bus was full, though, and when a white person got on the bus, Parks was told to stand up so the other person could take her seat. She refused and was arrested.

Hearing of Parks's courage, almost every African American living in Montgomery gathered to support her. Led by Dr. Martin Luther King Jr. and other leaders, 40,000 African Americans boycotted (refused to ride) the buses until the bus segregation laws were changed. The boycott lasted over a year until the United States Supreme Court ruled that segregation laws on public transportation were against the Constitution.

In the years following this successful challenge, Parks continued to work to support civil rights. She established the Rosa and Raymond Parks Institute for Self-Development that took groups of teenagers on civil rights tours.

Rosa Parks received many awards and honors. In 1996, President Clinton presented her with the Medal of Freedom. In 1999, she was honored with a Congressional Gold Medal. Known as the Mother of the Civil Rights Movement, thousands of people lined up to pay their respects at her death when her casket was placed in the Rotunda at the U.S. Capitol in 2005.

Segregation in Schools

Before Rosa Parks's arrest, the NAACP and other groups had already been trying to change the segregation laws concerning schools. The law of the land said "separate but equal" education was constitutional. However, the conditions in schools were never equal. Schools for African Americans were filled with used, old equipment. These school buildings were often in poor condition because not as much money was spent for these schools as was spent on schools for whites.

The NAACP worked hard to change these conditions. In 1954, an important case was taken to the Supreme Court by several NAACP lawyers, including Thurgood Marshall. (Thurgood Marshall eventually went on to become the first African American Supreme Court justice.) In this case, the NAACP tried to get a student named Linda Brown into a segregated school for whites. The lawyers proved that the school board spent more money on the school for white children.

A major victory came when the Supreme Court reversed its earlier decision and ruled that separate schools were not equal. They ordered all schools to open their doors to both blacks and whites as quickly as possible. With this decision came renewed hope that more equal rights could be won by taking cases to court.

On November 14, 1960, public schools were integrated in New Orleans, Louisiana. This day was especially important for one courageous little girl named Ruby Bridges. It was her first day in first grade. Federal marshals had to walk with her into William Frantz School to protect her from the angry mobs gathered to protest the integration. She spent the year alone with her teacher in an empty classroom because the other white children had been pulled out of the school by their parents.

When the next year of school started, parents finally sent their children back to school because they were not being educated. White and black students attended school together from then on. Ruby Bridges grew up and raised her own children, and has focused her energy to help improve education. She developed the Ruby Bridges Foundation to help train parents to take an active role in the education of their children.

Carry a Card Supporting Nonviolence

As one of the most important leaders during the Civil Rights Movement, Dr. Martin Luther King Jr. spent many years studying ways to bring changes to the nation without using violence. He combined his strong beliefs in Christianity with the teachings of Mahatma Gandhi, who brought great change to India without using violence. Dr. King believed it was important for African Americans to overcome years of racial hatred by using love and nonviolence. Dr. King believed that love was stronger than hate and would eventually win the battle for equal rights through peaceful means.

Many people and groups followed Dr. King's example of using nonviolence. One group called the Congress of Racial Equality (CORE) encouraged its members to carry a card in their pockets that listed ways to follow their commitment for nonviolence. Each card listed basic things to remember, such as to stay friendly and use good manners at all times, to not hit someone back if they were hit, to not laugh at other people, and to remember to love people and to use nonviolence.

You can try to learn how to use nonviolence, just as many students and other people did during the Civil Rights Movement. People were trained how to use nonviolence, and you can practice learning how to use it, too. One way to do this is to make a card to carry in your pocket listing nonviolent ideas on how to handle problems, just as members of CORE did.

Materials
Scrap paper
Index card
Pen or marker

On a piece of scrap paper, write down different ideas you have for handling problems in nonviolent ways, just as people tried to do during the Civil Rights Movement. Talk with your friends and write down their ideas, too. Include things such as:

* If someone yells at you, do not yell back.
* Speak calmly even if you are angry.
* If someone tries to get you to join a fight, turn and walk away.

After you have a list of ideas, choose five or six ideas that are the best ideas for you. Write these

Freedom Summer

During the summer of 1964, members of the Civil Rights Movement organized a special project that became known as Freedom Summer. During this summer, groups were organized to set up Freedom Schools throughout the South. African Americans of all ages were taught reading and math skills in the Freedom Schools. By learning how to read and write, they were able to pass tests and register to vote. They were taught about the United States Constitution and how to stand up for their rights as American citizens.

down on an index card. Carry the card in your pocket. The next time you are facing a problem, pull out your card and read through these ideas. Choose one idea to put into action so you can begin to solve your problems using nonviolence.

The Sit-In Movement and Freedom Rides

During the Civil Rights Movement, many people decided to join together to protest segregation. One group that formed was called the Student Nonviolent Coordinating Committee (SNCC). This group was run by students and was formed to organize sit-

Dr. Martin Luther King Jr. (1929-1968)

Dr. Martin Luther King Jr. was the most important leader in the Civil Rights Movement during the 1960s. He encouraged people to use nonviolence to bring changes to everyday life for African Americans. He organized countless boycotts, marches, and peaceful demonstrations. His speeches inspired hundreds of thousands of people to join together to work toward equal rights for everyone living in America. Dr. Martin Luther King Jr.'s most famous speech was given during the March on Washington in 1963. In this "I Have a Dream" speech, he shared his dream of black boys and girls joining hands with white boys and girls as brothers and sisters in America.

He won the Nobel Peace Prize and many other awards for his commitment to bringing important changes through peaceful ways. The world was very sad when this great man was assassinated in 1968. His wife, Coretta Scott King, and their four children continued to be strong voices in the struggle for civil rights.

ins as nonviolent ways to bring about integration in such places as restaurants, bathrooms, parks, and schools. During a sit-in, people who supported the Civil Rights Movement, black and white alike, calmly sat together in places where African Americans weren't allowed to sit. Also, SNCC made the goal to help all African Americans register to vote.

As students held sit-ins, newspaper reporters took their pictures and wrote about their stories. People across the nation learned, some for the first time, what was happening. More and more people began to support equal rights for everyone, putting pressure on stores and other businesses to change their ways. Soon lunch counters and many other public places became integrated.

Students who called themselves Freedom Riders decided to ride buses across different states in the South to test if bus companies in each state were allowing integration in the waiting areas and on buses.

Children Helped Change a Nation

One of the most memorable events during the Civil Rights Movement was when little children in Birmingham, Alabama, joined together to try to help bring integration to their city. Thousands of elementary and high school children participated in the events that became known as the Children's Crusade.

In the spring of 1963, Dr. King arrived in Birmingham, Alabama, where he set up daily workshops to teach people how to use nonviolence. Every night large meetings were held at the Sixteenth Street Baptist Church. Dr. King and other leaders spoke at these church meetings. Prayers were said and freedom songs were sung.

The Children's Crusade began on May 2 when suddenly, hundreds of children began marching out of the Sixteenth Street Baptist Church. Some children were as young as six years old. Over the next couple of days, thousands of school children marched out of the church and tried to walk downtown where they were not allowed to go. Police

Coretta Scott King
(1927-2006)

Coretta Scott King grew up in Alabama, experiencing segregation first hand. She graduated at the top of her high school class and went on to earn her degrees in music and education. After marrying Dr. Martin Luther King Jr., Mrs. King joined her husband in the Civil Rights Movement. She organized and performed in Freedom Concerts to tell the story of the Civil Rights Movement through poetry and song. Together she joined her husband to march side by side in demonstrations and travel throughout the nation and around the world as ambassadors of peace. After Dr. King's assassination, Mrs. King continued the dream she and her husband shared. She stayed at the forefront of the Civil Rights Movement, speaking at important places such as St. Paul's Cathedral in London and Harvard. Mrs. King and her four children built the Martin Luther King Jr. Center for Nonviolent Social Change. Its libraries hold the largest collection of books and material from the Civil Rights Movement. She also made it her goal to establish Dr. King's birthday, January 15, as a national holiday. She is remembered as the First Lady of Civil Rights.

arrested hundreds of little children by loading them onto school buses and taking them to jail. When the jail got full, the children were arrested and bused to the local fairground.

Reporters took many pictures of the police fighting against the little children by spraying them with powerful fire hoses and using attack dogs. Citizens all over America watched the terrible events on television or read about them in newspapers.

Eventually, several committees met to discuss changes in Birmingham. It was agreed that Birmingham would begin to integrate different parts of

Malcolm X
(1925-1965)

Malcolm X spoke out openly against Dr. Martin Luther King Jr.'s use of nonviolence. Some African Americans felt that nonviolence wasn't bringing changes fast enough. Malcolm X stood as a hero to these people who supported the idea of fighting for equal rights. Because of his viewpoints, he was one of the most controversial people of his time. Born in Nebraska as Malcolm Little, his father was killed by the Ku Klux Klan, and he grew up with a hatred for all whites. After living a life of crime, he learned about the black Muslim movement while in prison. It was during this time that he changed his name to Malcolm X and became a minister in the Nation of Islam. Malcolm X traveled to many places, giving fiery speeches about the rights and pride of African Americans. During his travels, he overcame his hatred for whites and began to speak about both races working together for civil rights. Before he could spread his new message of togetherness, he was assassinated while giving a speech in New York City.

the city over a period of 90 days. The children were released from jail, some of them having stayed there at least seven days.

The children who participated in the Children's Crusade not only helped change the segregation laws in Birmingham, Alabama, but they also inspired other people in other cities to work toward more civil rights for African Americans. Wave after wave of people in city after city across the nation followed the example of the children in Birmingham to try to change harmful segregation laws.

Make a Hand Fan

As people marched or joined in sit-ins, it often became very hot and uncomfortable. A common sight during these gatherings were simple hand fans. Not only did these hand fans provide some relief from the hot sun, but they also were a form of advertisement. They were printed with encouraging words, information about the event, or pictures of such civil rights leaders as Dr. Martin Luther King Jr. You can design a hand fan that is similar to the ones people carried during the Civil Rights Movement.

Materials

Illustration of fan

Tracing paper

Pencil

Scissors

Poster board

Markers or colored pencils

Jumbo craft stick

Stapler

Trace the outline of the fan onto the tracing paper. Cut this out and use it as a pattern to cut a fan from the poster board. Draw a picture of Dr. King on one side of the poster board. Write encouraging words across the top such as "We Shall Overcome." Staple the craft stick to the poster board to form the handle of the fan. Wave the fan gently back and forth in front of your face. Feel the refreshing breeze. Imagine how good it felt across the faces of the people who were marching along a road during the Civil Rights Movement on a hot, sunny day.

The March on Washington

Civil rights leaders decided to organize a march on Washington to urge that schools be integrated quickly throughout the country, to help pass a bill to lower unemployment for African Americans, and to help get a new Civil Rights Act passed in Congress. Civil rights groups and churches across the nation sent out flyers and informational brochures inviting people to join the march by going to Washington, D.C., on August 28, 1963. President John F. Kennedy supported the march.

More than 250,000 people joined in the march, making it the largest civil rights gathering in the history of the United States! Throughout the day, meetings were held, entertainment was provided, and many speeches were made. Dr. Martin Luther King Jr. gave his most famous speech, "I Have a Dream." In this important speech, Dr. King called for love, freedom, and hope for all people in America through racial unity. A peaceful and powerful demonstration, the March on Washington was a total success.

Carry a Sign

Many people carried signs during the March on Washington. These signs had words written on them stating things people cared about. Some of the signs said:

* We Will March as Long as We Can and Demand the Rights of Every Man
* We March for Jobs for All Now!
* America Has a Century-Old Debt to Pay Contracted on Emancipation Day
* No U.S. Dough to Help Jim Crow Grow
* We March for Integrated Schools Now!
* God of Justice, God of Power, Can America Deny Freedom in This Hour?

You can make a sign about something you care about. As you carry or display your sign, others will know what's important to you.

Materials
Poster board

Markers

Paint-stirring stick (available at hardware stores)

Glue

Stapler

Think about something that is important to you, such as helping people learn to read, taking turns in line, giving food to the homeless, or caring properly for pets. On the poster board, use the markers to write a slogan, or short saying, about this topic. Glue or staple a paint-stirring stick to the sign as a handle. Carry or display your sign so that others may see it. Give a speech explaining more fully what you are trying to say.

The issue of civil rights affected everyone in America. Whether living in wealth or poverty, whether living in the South or North, whether grown up or still a child, every American was challenged to bring equal rights to people of all races and situations.

8
Hope for Today and a Better Tomorrow

The success of the March on Washington showed Americans that many people supported the Civil Rights Movement. Sadly, however, President John F. Kennedy was shot and killed on November 22, 1963. Vice President Lyndon Johnson stepped in as the new president. President Johnson immediately called for Congress to quickly pass the new Civil Rights Bill. He also later signed the Voting Rights Act, an important new law that made it possible for African Americans to vote in places they hadn't been able to vote before because of discrimination. President Johnson also appointed African Americans as members of his political team, including Thurgood Marshall as the first black United States Supreme Court justice.

In 1968, Dr. Martin Luther King Jr. was shot and killed. Mourners lined the streets for the funeral procession to pay their respects to this outstanding leader. The world was shocked and saddened by the news, but people took courage in their efforts to continue Dr. King's great work for human rights.

The Civil Rights Movement had influenced the entire nation. Because of its impact, African Americans developed a national pride, and hope grew strong for the future. African Americans were voted into office and began to hold powerful positions in government. Many court cases were brought before the Supreme Court to permanently end segregation in schools and public places.

President Ronald Reagan signed a bill in 1983 to make Dr. Martin Luther King Jr.'s birthday a federal holiday. On January 15, 1986, Dr. King's birthday was celebrated for the first time. Dr. King was the first person to be honored in this way who wasn't a president of the United States. Ever since that first celebration, the citizens of America join together each year to honor the life and work of this important leader of the Civil Rights Movement.

Dedicated Historians

Carter Woodson carried the torch started many years earlier when historians such as James W. C. Pennington and William C. Nell devoted hours of research to write books and articles about important people and events in African American history. Woodson was passionate about honoring African American achievements and celebrating this rich history all throughout America.

Over the years, other historians have dedicated their lives to finding out more about America's past and the important role African Americans continue to contribute to the success of this nation. Historian Charles H. Wesley studied at such prestigious universities as Howard, Fisk, and Yale, receiving his doctorate from Harvard. He was president of Central State University and a professor and dean at Howard. He was also the director of the Association for the Study of Afro-American Life and History. He published many books about African American history.

Benjamin Quarles conducted extensive research on African Americans' participation in the American Revolution and the Civil War. His books about Frederick Douglass, Abraham Lincoln, John Brown, and black abolitionists explored the important influence of blacks in America regarding the issues of slavery and equal rights. A university professor, he taught history for many years. Through his numerous articles and books on black history, Quarles established a foundation for American historians today.

Modern day historians such as Lerone Bennett Jr., Darlene Clark Hine, Jessie Carney Smith, and Henry Louis Gates Jr. continue to write monumental books about the milestones and achievements of African Americans. Using sources such as journals, personal letters, war records, and newspaper articles, these historians have uncovered amazing facts and details about the history of blacks in America.

A New African American Renaissance

Following the years of influence and change brought about through the Civil Rights Movement, African Americans continued to grow as a strong presence,

Carter Woodson
(1875-1950)

Carter Woodson is known as the father of African American history. Born to parents who had lived during the time of slavery, he was not able to attend school until he was 20 years old. When he did go to school, however, he was able to earn his high school diploma in just two years! Woodson then attended Harvard, where he received his PhD. Concerned that there were no books at the time that contained information about the history of African Americans, Woodson wrote numerous books and edited a journal about important historical contributions made by African Americans. In 1927, he began observing Negro History Week to make information about African Americans available to people everywhere. This week was officially expanded into Black History Month in 1976, which is still celebrated every February.

Maya Angelou
(1928-)

Maya Angelou is a well-known poet and author who includes rich portrayals of African American women in her work. Born in St. Louis, Missouri, she grew up in Arkansas where she lived with her grandmother (a time that she writes about in *I Know Why the Caged Bird Sings*, the first of five autobiographical novels). After graduating from high school, she worked as a magazine editor, poet, novelist, and actress. She has received many prestigious awards and honors for her work including delivering her poem "On the Pulse of Morning" at the inauguration of President Clinton in 1993.

In politics, Shirley Chisholm was elected to the U.S. House of Representatives in 1968 and became the first African American woman in Congress. In 2005, Barack Obama became the fifth African American to serve in the Senate, following the trail blazed by Hiram Revels, Blanche Bruce, Edward Brooke, and Carol Moseley Braun. Many African Americans became mayors of major cities, such as Thomas Bradley, who was elected mayor of Los Angeles, California. Men and women rose to influential positions—Brigadier General (Ret.) Clara Adams-Ender was the highest-ranking woman in the U.S. Army, and Vernon Jordan was a key advisor to President Bill Clinton. Astronauts such as "Guy" Bluford, Ronald McNair, and Mae Jemison reached for the stars as they explored outer space.

In business, achievements were made by people heading multimillion-dollar enterprises. John H. Johnson established the magazines *Ebony* and *Jet*. Carl Ware became senior vice president of the Coca-Cola Company. In sports, African American superstars who scored record-breaking achievements, such as Jackie Joyner-Kersee and Michael

voice, and identity in America. They achieved important milestones in politics, business, sports, faith, education, civil rights, and the arts.

Sarah Louise Delany
(1889-1999)
and
Anne Elizabeth Delany
(1891-1995)

Sarah Delany received her bachelor's and master's degrees from Columbia University. She integrated New York City's school system as the first appointed African American high school home economics teacher. Elizabeth Delany became the second licensed AfricanAmerican woman dentist in New York City. She shared a dentist office with her brother in the center of Harlem, where their patients included famous African American performers, artists, and political leaders. The office was also a center for political activists, including W. E. B. Du Bois, who worked for civil rights.

Both sisters lived for more than 100 years. During their lifetimes they experienced Jim Crow segregation laws, both World Wars, integration of sports and other institutions, and the Civil Rights Movement. The story of their lives, *Having Our Say: The Delany Sisters' First 100 Years*, became a bestseller and was adapted for the stage.

Jordan, inspired every American sports-minded youth to go for the gold.

Motown music's catchy songs swept the nation with top hits by artists such as Smokey Robinson, Stevie Wonder, and Diana Ross and the Supremes. Alvin Ailey and Arthur Mitchell explored the use of African and African American dance tradition in various styles such as ballet and modern dance. Trumpet player Wynton Marsalis, a modern day jazz musician, brought jazz to the world through his

Oprah Winfrey
(1954-)

As host of the talk show *The Oprah Winfrey Show*, Oprah Winfrey became one of the best-known personalities in America. She was one of only three women in the television industry to own her own production studio. Rising up out of a troubled childhood to win numerous honors and awards, Winfrey has used her influential position to promote literacy, help abused children, encourage volunteerism, and launch numerous civic programs.

countless musical programs as director of jazz at Lincoln Center. A musical genius, Marsalis was the first jazz musician to win a Pulitzer Prize, for his composition "Blood on the Fields."

Romare Beardon expressed the complex emotions of the Civil Rights Movement through his

unique art. Authors such as Alex Haley, Toni Morrison, and Alice Walker won numerous awards. Rita Dove was named poet laureate of the United States.

General Colin Luther Powell
(1937-)

General Colin Powell has become one of the most respected men in the nation. He demonstrated wise leadership skills in times of difficult military crises during the invasion of Panama and the Persian Gulf War. As a four-star general he was selected to be chairman of the Joint Chiefs of Staff, the highest military post in the United States. His autobiography was published after his retirement, establishing him as a bestselling author. Powell is a hero for all Americans.

Condoleezza Rice (1954-)

Born in Birmingham, Alabama, the center stage of the Civil Rights Movement, Condoleezza Rice's parents tried to shield her from the Jim Crow segregation laws of the South. When a bomb exploded in the Sixteenth Street Baptist Church from racist violence, however, one of her friends was killed. She never forgot that day. Not wanting to become bitter from the struggles they faced, Rice's parents taught her that education was an important way to overcome racism. Extremely intelligent, Rice excelled in school. Playing the piano, ice skating, and sports were also hobbies she enjoyed. Always interested in politics, she became a political science professor at Stanford University, where she won many awards and held important positions. Serving in Washington, D.C., Rice became the national security advisor. In 2005, Rice was appointed the secretary of state for the United States of America, where many considered her one of the most powerful women in the world.

There were so many award-winning books, theater productions, music, and other art forms produced expressing the African American experience that many people have called this the second African American Renaissance.

All-Star Athletes

In recent history, many African American athletes have reached new heights and set new records by impressing cheering crowds with their ability, strength, endurance, and skill. So many outstanding men and women have achieved victory after victory in various sports events that magazines and news reports frequently feature the profiles of these key players. Truly these legendary sports figures have become heroes for every boy and girl in America as well as throughout the world. African Americans have also become umpires, coaches, managers, and directors overseeing major teams.

Basketball

* Bill Russell led the Boston Celtics as one of the best all-time players. He became the first black coach of a National Basketball Association (NBA) team.
* Kareem Abdul-Jabbar become the top scorer in the NBA.
* Wilt Chamberlain was the only NBA player to ever score 100 points in one basketball game.
* Magic Johnson joined the Los Angeles Lakers as a star player, earning the highest paid contract ever signed in the history of sports.

Michael Jordan
(1963-)

Many people consider Michael Jordan to be the greatest basketball player of all time. Born in Brooklyn, New York, Jordan excelled at baseball as a youth, and he didn't join the high school basketball team until he was a sophomore. He attended basketball camps and practiced hard with his brother Larry in order to become a better player. During college at the University of North Carolina, he won national recognition when he helped lead his team to the national championship. He went on to play basketball in the Olympic games and became a superstar player for the Chicago Bulls. Jordan helped lead his team to six NBA championships and earned five NBA Most Valuable Player awards. Jordan is a role model for American youth to succeed in pursuing their dreams.

* Michael Jordan led the Chicago Bulls to many NBA championships, frequently receiving the Most Valuable Player (MVP) award.
* Shaquille O'Neal was one of NBA's star players, electrifying the crowds as he took the Los Angeles Lakers on the road to numerous championships. In his first season with the Miami Heat, he also led them to become the new champions of the NBA.

Baseball

* Hank Aaron broke Babe Ruth's record of 714 home runs and retired with a total of 755.
* Roberto Clemente was honored on a U.S. postage stamp for his all-star career with the Pittsburgh Pirates.
* Reggie Jackson amazed crowds during World Series games where he tied or set seven new records.
* Ricky Henderson stole more bases than any other player in the major leagues.
* Tony Gwynn was a batting champion for the San Diego Padres and went on to become the head coach of San Diego State University's baseball team. He was inducted into the Hall of Fame in 2007.
* Barry Bonds' powerful home runs racked up his stats to become the second player in history to pass Babe Ruth's record, causing baseball fans to eagerly watch this outstanding player's career.

Football

* Jim Brown led the National Football League (NFL) with season and career total rushing yards to become one of the most famous athletes of the 20th century.
* Gale Sayers astounded fans with his unbelievable agility and quick moves on the field, earning top points in his short career. He was named the 1965 Rookie of the Year.
* O. J. Simpson won the 1968 Heisman Trophy while playing for the University of Southern California. He won numerous awards and set a record for the number of rushing yards in a single game.

* Walter Payton of the Chicago Bears broke Jim Brown's and O. J. Simpson's rushing records to become the NFL's all-time leader in rushing yards.
* Jerry Rice made more touchdowns during his NFL career than any other player.
* Deion Sanders played in the Super Bowl during his football career and in the World Series during his career in baseball.

Boxing

* "Sugar Ray" Robinson was one of the greatest athletes in the history of boxing, winning numerous world titles.
* "Sugar Ray" Leonard earned more money in his exciting championship career than any other boxer before him.
* Joe Frazier boxed against George Foreman and Muhammad Ali in some of the most thrilling heavyweight championship matches of the 20th century.

* George Foreman boxed in legendary heavyweight matches against Joe Frazier and Muhammad Ali. After retirement, he became a successful businessman, then returned to the ring for more sensational matches and championship victories.
* Muhammad Ali was the first boxer to win the world heavyweight title three times. He was known for his quick moves in the ring and outgoing media personality.
* Mike Tyson's powerful punch launched him to fame as he won the world heavyweight championship.

Golf

* Charlie Sifford was the first African American to win a major professional golf tournament and was the first black golfer admitted to the Professional Golfers Association (PGA).
* Lee Elder was the first African American to qualify to play in the PGA Masters Tournament.

* Calvin Peete won more victories on the PGA tour than any other golfer in the early 1980s in spite of a childhood arm injury that affected his golf swing.
* Tiger Woods accomplished many firsts and set amazing records on his way to becoming one of the best all-time golfers and winning his way into the hearts and homes of sports fans around the globe.

Tennis

* Althea Gibson skillfully earned her position as the best woman tennis player in the world, achieving many firsts and winning numerous awards.
* Arthur Ashe rose victoriously through the ranks to win the World Championship Tennis singles title, even though many tennis courts and tournaments were segregated in the early years of his career.

* Zina Garrison was one of the top players in women's tennis during the 1980s.
* Venus and Serena Williams became two of the youngest tennis stars in America when these sisters started winning matches on the courts.

Track and Field

* Wilma Rudolph overcame a childhood physical disability to become the first woman track star to win three gold medals in the Olympics.
* Edwin Moses kept beating his own track records in hurdles during years of an unbelievable winning streak where no other runner could beat him.
* Carl Lewis won four gold medals in track and field in the 1984 Olympics.
* Jackie Joyner-Kersee won a total of six medals in the Olympics, earning her a reputation as an outstanding athlete.

* Florence Griffith-Joyner was a popular favorite. She was known by her fans as Flo-Jo, the fastest woman in the world.

Miscellaneous Sports

* Cheryl Miller dominated the scoreboard as she led her team to championship victories in women's basketball.
* Diane Durham and Dominique Dawes displayed their skill on the balance beam, bars, floor, and vault events to win numerous competitions in gymnastics.
* Debi Thomas achieved many firsts as she won the United States and world figure skating championships and an Olympic medal in ice skating.
* Grant Fuhr was the first African American drafted into the National Hockey League.
* Vonetta Flowers became the first African American to win a gold medal in the Winter Olympics. In 2002, she raced to her Olympic victory in a bobsled.

* Briana Scurry was a number-one goalkeeper in women's soccer.
* Cheryl White took her place in the history of horse racing as the first woman jockey.
* Donna Creck was inducted into the Women's Sport Hall of Fame for horse riding.
* Charles Sampson, a modern cowboy, won a world championship in rodeo.

Kwanzaa

In 1966, Kwanzaa (say it: KWAHN-zah) was first celebrated in Los Angeles, California, by Dr. Maulana Karenga, a professor of black studies, with his family and friends. With the vision of introducing a special holiday to celebrate the cultural heritage of African Americans, Dr. Karenga created Kwanzaa. More and more families celebrate Kwanzaa each year.

Practice Swahili

Dr. Karenga decided to use the language of Swahili (say it: swah-HE-lee) for the celebration of Kwanzaa. He chose Swahili because it is an African language that's not limited to one specific group. In Swahili, Kwanzaa means "the first fruits of the harvest." Dr. Karenga developed Kwanzaa to use the theme of the harvest as a way to celebrate each year's unity, growth, and success of a better life for African Americans. He developed Kwanzaa as a seven-day celebration that starts on December 26 and ends on January 1. He chose seven symbols to be used to celebrate Kwanzaa. He also chose seven principles or themes to focus on during this important holiday.

During the celebration of Kwanzaa, there are many important Swahili words used. You can practice saying these words and learn their meanings, too.

The Seven Principles of Kwanzaa

* Umoja (say it: oom-OH-jah) means unity
* Kujichagulia (say it: koo-jee-chah-GOO-lee-ah) means self-determination
* Ujima (say it: oo-JEE-mah) means responsibility to work together
* Ujamaa (say it: oo-JAH-mah) means supporting each other in business
* Nia (say it: NEE-ah) means purpose
* Kuumba (say it: koo-OOM-bah) means creativity
* Imani (say it: ee-MAH-nee) means faith

The Seven Symbols of Kwanzaa

* Mazao (say it: mah-ZAH-oh) means fruits, vegetables, and nuts
* Mkeka (say it: muh-KAY-kah) means straw place mat
* Kinara (say it: kee-NAH-rah) means candle holder

- Mishumaa (say it: mee-SHOO-ma-ah) means seven candles
- Muhindi (say it: moo-HEEN-dee) means ears of corn
- Zawadi (say it: sah-WAH-dee) means gifts
- Kikombe Cha Umoja (say it: kee-COMB-bay chah oom-OH-jah) means the cup of unity

The Symbols of Kwanzaa

During the actual celebration of Kwanzaa, seven important symbols are used. These symbols are used to help understand the seven principles, or themes, of Kwanzaa. They are also used as a way to remember important events of African American history and teach these to the next generation of children.

On each day of the weeklong holiday, the seven symbols are displayed and used as the seven principles are taught and discussed. When the holiday is finished, however, the principles of Kwanzaa can be followed throughout the year.

Fruits, Vegetables, and Nuts

Fruits, vegetables, and nuts are symbols of the harvest. The harvest in Africa was often celebrated with much rejoicing. A great sense of accomplishment was felt by all the people in all the different tribes. Today, the fruits and vegetables displayed during Kwanzaa show honor to African American workers and the good job they've done throughout the past year. This display also honors the children and their accomplishments.

The Place Mat

The place mat is usually made from straw or fabric. It is placed at the center of the display for Kwanzaa and all the other symbols are set upon it. The place mat symbolizes the history of African Americans. It is upon this important history that all present and future accomplishments are built.

The Candle Holder

The candle holder is the base that holds the seven candles. It repre- sents the strength that unites all seven princi-ples of Kwanzaa into one symbol. The candle holder stands for the one main source from which all seven principles come.

The Seven Candles

There are three red candles, one black candle, and three green candles used during Kwanzaa. The three red candles are on the left, the black candle is in the center, and the three green candles are on the right. Each color has its own meaning. The red stands for the struggle African Americans have experienced as they gained free-dom and equal rights. The black stands for the unity of all African Americans. The green stands for the hope African Americans cherish for the future.

The Ear of Corn

An ear of corn is put on the place mat for each child in the family or each child who participates in the feast of Kwanzaa. Children are very important to the celebration of Kwanzaa. They represent the happiness of today. Children also symbolize new life and hope for the future.

Gifts

On the last day of Kwanzaa, special gifts are given to the children. Most gifts are homemade as a symbol of the creative abilities of the members of the family. These gifts repre-sent the success of the parents through the last year, as well as the success and accomplishments of the children.

The Cup of Unity

A special cup is placed on the place mat to represent unity. During the celebration, wine or juice from the cup of unity is shared by all present. It symbolizes the unity of all present and those from the past.

Celebrate Kwanzaa

The celebration of Kwanzaa begins on December 26 and lasts for seven days. You can celebrate it with your family and friends, just as many people do in the United States today.

December 26

Everyone greets each other by asking "Habari gani?" (Say it: hah-bah-ree GAH-nee.) This means, "What is the news?" Today, you answer by saying, "Umoja" (say it: oom-OH-jah). During the celebration, the black candle in the center is lit. Often, a child is chosen each day to light the candle. Everyone drinks from the cup of unity. African Americans from the past are honored. Today's focus is unity.

December 27

Everyone greets each other by asking "Habari gani?" (Say it: hah-bah-ree GAH-nee.) Today, you answer by saying, "Kujichagulia" (Say it: koo-jee-chah-GOO-lee-ah). The black candle and a red candle are lit. Everyone drinks from the cup of unity. African Americans from the past are honored. Today's focus is self-determination.

December 28

Everyone greets each other by asking "Habari gani?" (Say it: hah-bah-ree GAH-nee.) Today, you answer by saying, "Ujima" (Say it: oo-JEE-mah). The black candle, a red candle, and a green candle are lit. Everyone drinks from the cup of unity. African Americans from the past are honored. Today's focus is the responsibility of working together.

December 29

Everyone greets each other by asking "Habari gani?" (Say it: hah-bah-ree GAH-nee.) Today, you answer by saying, "Ujamaa" (say it: oo-JAH-mah). The black candle, two red candles, and a green candle are lit. Everyone drinks from the cup of unity. African Americans from the past are honored. Today's focus is supporting each other in business.

December 30

Everyone greets each other by asking "Habari gani?" (Say it: hah-bah-ree GAH-nee.) Today, you answer by saying, "Nia" (say it: NEE-ah). The black candle, two red candles, and two green candles are lit. Everyone drinks from the cup of unity. African Americans from the past are honored. Today's focus is purpose.

December 31

Everyone greets each other by asking "Habari gani?" (Say it: hah-bah-ree GAH-nee.) Today, you answer by saying, "Kuumba" (say it: koo-OOM-bah). The black candle, three red candles, and two green candles are lit. Everyone drinks from the cup of unity. African Americans from the past are honored. Today's focus is creativity.

On this day a special feast is held. The feast is usually held in the evening. There are many favorite dishes to share. Music, dance, folktales, and special memories are often enjoyed.

January 1

Everyone greets each other by asking "Habari gani?" (Say it: hah-bah-ree GAH-nee.) Today, you answer by saying, "Imani" (say it: ee-MAH-nee). The black candle, three red candles, and three green candles are lit. Everyone drinks from the cup of unity. African Americans from the past are honored. Today's focus is faith.

On this day the gifts are given. Each member's accomplishments from the past year are acknowledged and honored. After the gifts are opened, the celebration of Kwanzaa draws to a close. Everyone shouts "Harambee!" (say it: hah-rahm-BEH)

seven times. This is a Swahili saying that means "Let's pull together."

Wear a Kufi

During the celebration of Kwanzaa, you might want to wear a kufi (say it: KOO-fee). A kufi is a round hat made from soft fabric with an African design. You can make a kufi from felt to wear during this important holiday.

Materials

Strips of red, yellow, black, and green felt,
   2 by 24 inches (5 by 61 cm)
Sharp scissors
Needle
Thread
8 safety pins

Wrap a black strip of felt around your head for the headband. Overlap the edges 1 inch (2.5 cm), cutting away the extra felt. Use a safety pin to hold the ends together. Use a needle and thread to stitch the headband together.

With the headband on your head, use a yellow strip to measure from one side of the headband, across the top of your head, and to the other side of the headband. Cut this strip to the correct length for the top of your hat. Cut one strip of red felt, green felt, and black felt to match the same length as the yellow strip. You should now have four shorter strips of felt.

Following the illustration as a guide, arrange the four felt strips so they overlap in the center like spokes on a wheel. Stitch through the center with your needle and thread. Use the safety pins to pin the edge of each felt strip around the headband so that all the strips are evenly spaced. Try on your kufi to see if it fits. Trim any strips that seem too long and adjust the safety pins as needed. Stitch each strip of felt to the headband, removing the safety pins as you go.

Joining Together for a Future of Hope

After the holiday of Kwanzaa is over and the celebrations are finished, the principles can still be followed throughout the year. These seven principles are becoming a way of life for many African Americans.

There is renewed pride, as African Americans celebrate individuality while appreciating a heritage rich in tradition and culture. Ancestors gave this generation a sense of dignity and strong determination, for they triumphed over years of hardships and inequality to emerge as a powerful presence in America.

It is the challenge of all kids to continue to build on and extend this rich inheritance.

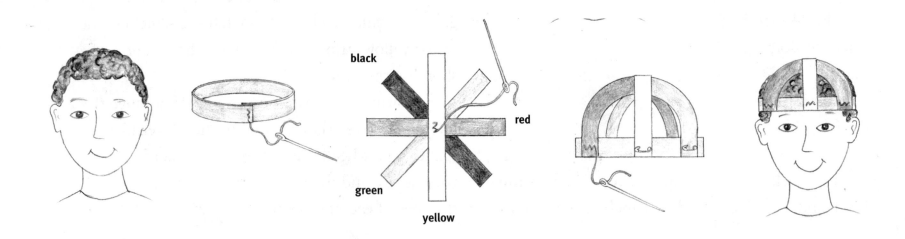

Suggested Reading List for Kids

Black Americans of Achievement series of biographies for children by Chelsea House Publishers.

Branch, Muriel. *Juneteenth: Freedom Day*. New York: Cobblehill Books, 1998.

Freedman, Russell. *Children of the Wild West*. New York: Clarion Books, 1983.

Green, Richard L., et al. *Black History at an Early Age: Volumes 1-10*. Chicago: Empak Publishing Company, 1993.

Green, Richard L., et al. *Documenting Our Own History: Empak Publishing Company Booklet Series Volumes 1-10*. Chicago: Empak Publishing Company, 1996.

Haskins, Jim. *The Day Martin Luther King, Jr., Was Shot: A Photo History of the Civil Rights Movement*. New York: Scholastic Inc., 1992.

Hopson, Dr. Darlene, and Dr. Derek Hopson. *Juba This & Juba That: 100 African-American Games for Children*. New York: Simon and Schuster, 1996.

McGowen, Tom. *African Americans in the Old West*. New York: Children's Press, 1998.

Mettger, Zak. *Reconstruction*. New York: Lodestar Books, 1994.

Myers, Walter. *Now Is Your Time! The African American Struggle for Freedom*. New York: Harper Collins Publishers, 1991.

Patrick, Diane. *Amazing African American History: A Book of Answers for Kids*. New York: John Wiley & Sons, Inc., 1998.

Steward, Jeffrey. *1001 Things Everyone Should Know About African American History*. New York: Doubleday, 1996.

Thomas, Velma Maia. *Lest We Forget: The Passage from Africa to Slavery and Emancipation*. New York: Crown Publishers, Inc., 1997.

Teacher Resources

Web Sites to Explore

Smithsonian Education: African American Heritage Teaching Resources
www.smithsonianeducation.org/educators/resource_library/african_american_resources.html

This Smithsonian site offers a rich wealth of resources covering the entire span of African American history. Some topics include classroom activities, guides, and reading lists.

Black Heritage Trail
www.afroammuseum.org/trail.htm

Boston's historic buildings on the Black Heritage Trail are featured on this site. Detailed background information, maps, and photographs are also included.

Digital History
www.digitalhistory.uh.edu/

This site has a list of primary sources about American history which highlights significant events from African American history as well. Among the many activities included, you can find out what happened on this day in history, watch videos, and print out classroom aids to use.

Documenting the American South
http://docsouth.unc.edu/

Visit this site to view original slave narratives and other important documents of southern culture and African American history otherwise available only in university archives. You can search through the alphabetical listings of authors or titles to find a specific book or document. It is sponsored by the University Library of the University of North Carolina at Chapel Hill.

Scholastic Research Tools: Martin Luther King, Jr. and African American History
http://teacher.scholastic.com/researchtools/articlearchives/honormlk/index.htm

Scholastic's site includes news articles, links, and reading lists about African American history for students and teachers to use.

NARA—For Educators and Students
www.archives.gov/education/

The National Archives has a Web site called the Digital Classroom. It includes lesson plans for using primary documents from its collections in the classroom. Teaching activities are correlated to national standards and include cross-curricular activities.

Africans in America
www.pbs.org/wgbh/aia

This Web site includes a printable teacher's guide to use as a companion to the Africans in America video series. It contains a wealth of information as well, even if you do not use the videos in your classroom. Featuring an overview of the entire scope of African American history, the site has many primary resources and photographs.

Education World: Special Theme: Black History
www.education-world.com/a_special/black_history.shtml

This site is geared to educators, with lesson plans, plays, activities, and projects to use during Black History Month. There are a variety of topics to use with various age groups.

African American Studies Toolkit
www.creativefolk.com/toolkit/home.html

Spanning the curriculum to include music, visual arts, math, and science, this site contains a wealth of information for teachers to use. There are links to explore, posters to buy, and lesson plans to use. There is even a link for travel guides to use while planning a visit to museums or important historical sites.

Black History Month
www.teachervision.fen.com/black-history-month-black-history/6602.html

Visitors to this site can print coloring pages, worksheets, quizzes and lesson plans for personal or classroom use. (Some features require membership.) Cross-curricular activities are included for such subjects as physical education, art, social studies, and math.

Books to Read

Altman, Susan. *The Encyclopedia of African-American Heritage*. New York: Facts on File, 1997.

Cantor, George. *Historic Landmarks of Black America*. Detroit: Gale Research Inc., 1991.

Hornsby, Alton Jr. *Chronology of African-American History*. Detroit: Gale Research Inc., 1991.

Smith, Sande. *Who's Who in African American History*. New York: Smithmark, 1994.

Selected Bibliography

Books

Abdul-Jabbar, Kareem. *Black Profiles in Courage*. New York: William Morrow and Company, Inc., 1996.

Abrahams, Roger. *Afro-American Folktales*. New York: Pantheon Books, 1985.

Adler, David. *A Picture Book of Harriet Tubman*. New York: Scholastic, 1992.

Adler, David. *A Picture Book of Jesse Owens*. New York: Scholastic, 1992.

"African Americans." *Microsoft Encarta Encyclopedia 2000*. Microsoft Corporation, 1993-1999.

Alexander, E. Curtis. *Richard Allen*. New York: ECA Associates, 1985.

Alexander, Rae, and Julius Lester. *Young and Black in America*. New York: Random House, 1970.

Altman, Susan. *The Encyclopedia of African-American Heritage*. New York: Facts on File, 1997.

"Ancient Civilization." *Compton's Encyclopedia Volume 1*. Chicago: Compton's Learning Company, 1992.

Anderson, David. *Kwanzaa: An Everyday Resource and Instructional Guide*. New York: Gumbs & Thomas Publishers, Inc., 1992.

"Angelou, Maya." *Microsoft Encarta Encyclopedia 2000*. Microsoft Corporation, 1993–1999.

Appiah, Kwame Anthony and Henry Louis Gates, Jr. *Africana*. New York: Basic Civitas Books, 1999.

Asante, Molefi, and Mark Mattson. *Historical and Cultural Atlas of African Americans*. New York: Simon and Schuster, 1992.

Ball, Edward. *Slaves in the Family*. New York: Farrar, Straus, and Giroux, 1998.

Baring-Gould, William, and Ceil Baring-Gould. *The Annotated Mother Goose*. New York: Bramhall House, 1962.

Benberry, Cuesta. *Always There: The African-American Presence in American Quilts*. Louisville, KY: The Kentucky Quilt Project, Inc., 1992.

Bennett, Lerone Jr. *Before the Mayflower: A History of Black America*. Chicago: Johnson Publishing Company, Inc., 1992.

Bernstein, Rebecca, et al. *Addy's Cook Book*. Middleton, WI: Pleasant Company, 1994.

Bial, Raymond. *The Underground Railroad*. New York: Houghton Mifflin, 1995.

Billington, Ray Allen, Ed. *The Journal of Charlotte L. Forten*. New York: W. W. Norton & Company, 1953.

Birnie, W. A. H., et al. *Reader's Digest Family Songbook*. Pleasantville, New York: The Reader's Digest Association, Inc., 1969.

Braasch, Barbara, et al. *Children's Crafts*. Menlo Park, CA: Lane Publishing, 1978.

Branch, Muriel. *Juneteenth: Freedom Day*. New York: Cobblehill Books, 1998.

Branch, Taylor. *Parting the Waters: America in the King Years 1954–63*. New York: Simon & Schuster Inc., 1988.

Brewster, Paul. *American Nonsinging Games*. Norman, OK: University of Oklahoma Press, 1953.

Buckley, Gail. *American Patriots*. New York: Random House, 2001.

Cantor, George. *Historic Landmarks of Black America*. Detroit: Gale Research Inc., 1991.

Chocolate, Deborah M. Newton. *My First Kwanzaa Book*. New York: Scholastic, 1992.

Ciment, James. *Atlas of African-American History*. New York: Checkmark Books, 2001.

Coffin, Tristram, and Hennig Cohen. *Folklore in America*. New York: Doubleday & Company, 1966.

Collins, Charles, and David Cohen. *The African Americans: A Celebration of Achievement*. New York: Penguin Books, 1995.

Compton's Encyclopedia, Volumes 1–26. Chicago: Compton's Learning Company, 1992.

Courlander, Harold. *A Treasure of Afro-American Folklore*. New York: Crown Publishers, 1976.

"Cowboy." *Compton's Encyclopedia*. Volume 5. Chicago: Compton's Learning Company, 1992.

Cox, Clinton. *Come All You Brave Soldiers: Blacks in the Revolutionary War*. New York: Scholastic, Inc., 2002.

Crew, Spencer. *Field to Factory*. Washington, DC: Smithsonian Institution, 1987.

Dallin, Leon, and Lynn Dallin. *Heritage Songster*. Dubuque, IA: Wm. C. Brown Company Publishers, 1966.

Delany, Sarah, and A. Elizabeth Delany with Amy Hearth. *Having Our Say*. New York: Dell Publishing, 1993.

Dramer, Kim. *Native Americans and Black Americans*. Philadelphia: Chelsea House Publishers, 1997.

Diamond, Arthur. *Prince Hall*. Philadelphia: Chelsea House Publishers, 1992.

Dodson, Howard, et al. *Jubilee*. Washington, DC: National Geographic, 2002.

Durlacher, Ed. *The Play Party Book*. New York: Devin-Adair Company, 1945.

"Egypt, Ancient." *Compton's Encyclopedia*. Volume 7. Chicago: Compton's Learning Company, 1992.

Emrich, Duncan. *The Nonsense Book of Riddles, Rhymes, Tongue Twisters, Puzzles, and Jokes from American Folklore*. New York: Four Winds Press, 1974.

Everett, Susanne. *History of Slavery*. Greenwich, CT: Chartwell Books, Inc., 1991.

Filler, Louis. *The Crusade Against Slavery*. New York: Harper and Row, 1960.

Franklin, John Hope, and Alfred Moss, Jr. *From Slavery to Freedom: A History of Negro Americans*. New York: McGraw-Hill, Inc., 1988.

Freedman, Russell. *Children of the Wild West*. New York: Clarion Books, 1983.

Freedman, Russell. *Lincoln: A Photobiography*. New York: Scholastic, 1987.

Gaines, Ernest. *The Autobiography of Miss Jane Pittman*. New York: Dial Press, 1974.

Garraty, John. *The American Nation*. New York: Harper & Row, 1966.

George, Carol V. R. *Segregated Sabbaths*. New York: Oxford University Press, 1973.

Gibbons, Gail. *Yippee-Yay!: A Book About Cowboys and Cowgirls*. New York: Little, Brown and Company, 1998.

Green, Richard L., et al. *Black History at an Early Age: Volumes I–X*. Chicago: Empak Publishing Company, 1993.

Green, Richard L., et al. *Documenting Our Own History: Empak Publishing Company Booklet Series Volumes I–X*. Chicago: Empak Publishing Company, 1996.

Green, Richard L., et al. *The Empak Black History Activity and Resource Guide*. Chicago: Empak Publishing Company, 1993.

Greenwood, Barbara. *A Pioneer Sampler*. Boston: Houghton Mifflin Company, 1994.

Grosvenor, Melville, Ed. *America's Historylands*. Washington, DC: National Geographic Society, 1962.

Hamilton, Sue L. *The Assassination of a Leader: Martin Luther King, Jr.* Minneapolis, MN: Abdo & Daughters, 1989.

Harley, Sharon. *The Timetables of African-American History*. New York: Simon & Schuster, 1995.

Haskins, Jim. *The Day Martin Luther King, Jr., Was Shot: A Photo History of the Civil Rights Movement*. New York: Scholastic Inc., 1992.

Hine, Darlene Clark. *Black Women in America: An Historical Encyclopedia*. Brooklyn, New York: Carlson Publishing Inc., 1993.

Hine, Darlene Clark. *Facts on File Encyclopedia of Black Women in America: The Early Years, 1619–1899*. New York: Facts on File, Inc. 1997.

Hine, Darlene Clark. *Facts on File Encyclopedia of Black Women in America: Literature*. New York: Facts on File, Inc., 1997.

Holloway, Joseph. *Africanisms in American Culture*. Bloomington, IN: Indiana University Press, 1990.

Hopson, Dr. Darlene, and Dr. Derek Hopson. *Juba This & Juba That*. New York: Simon and Schuster, 1996.

Hunt, W. Ben. *The Complete Book of Indian Crafts and Lore*. New York: Golden Press, 1968.

Hunter, Ilene, and Marilyn Judson. *Simple Folk Instruments to Make and to Play*. New York: Simon and Schuster, 1977.

Johnson, Charles, and Patricia Smith, et al. *Africans in America: America's Journey Through Slavery*. New York: Harcourt Brace & Company, 1998.

Jones, Bessie, and Bess Lomax Hawes. *Step It Down: Games, Plays, Songs, and Stories from the Afro-American Heritage*. New York: Harper and Row, 1972.

"Jordan, Michael." *Microsoft Encarta Encyclopedia 2000*. Microsoft Corporation, 1993–1999.

Kalman, Bobbie. *Life on a Plantation*. New York: Crabtree Publishing Company, 1997.

Kaplan, Sidney and Emma Nogrady Kaplan. *The Black Presence in the Era of the American Revolution*. Amherst: The University of Massachusetts Press, 1989.

Katz, William. *Eyewitness*. New York: Simon and Schuster, 1995.

Katz, William. *The Black West*. New York: Simon and Schuster, 1996.

King, Coretta Scott. *My Life with Martin Luther King, Jr.* New York: Holt Rinehart and Winston, 1969.

Klagsbrun, Francine. *Freedom Now!: The Story of the Abolitionists*. Boston: Houghton Mifflin Company, 1972.

Klots, Steve. *Richard Allen*. New York: Chelsea House Publishers, 1991.

Leckie, Robert. *The Wars of America*. New York: Harper & Row, 1968.

Lester, Julius. *More Tales of Uncle Remus*. New York: Dial Books, 1988.

Lester, Julius. *The Last Tales of Uncle Remus*. New York: Dial Books, 1994.

Levenson, Dorothy. *The First Book of the Civil War*. New York: Franklin Watts, Inc., 1968.

Levine, Ellen. *Freedom's Children*. New York: Avon Books, 1993.

Levine, Ellen. *If You Lived at the Time of Martin Luther King*. NY: Scholastic Inc., 1990.

Loewenbert, Bert James and Ruth Bogin. *Black Women in Nineteenth-Century American Life*. University Park: The Pennsylvania State University Press, 1976.

Lomax, Alan. *The Folk Songs of North America*. Garden City, NY: Dolphin Books, 1975.

Lyons, Mary E. *Master of Mahogany: Tom Day, Free Black Cabinetmaker*. New York: Charles Scribner's Sons, 1994.

Malone, Jacqui. *Steppin' on the Blues*. Chicago: University of Illinois Press, 1996.

Mathews, Marcia M. *Richard Allen*. Baltimore: Helicon, 1963.

McGowen, Tom. *African-Americans in the Old West*. New York: Children's Press, 1998.

McMickle, Marvin A. *An Encyclopedia of African American Christian Heritage*. Valley Forge: Judson Press, 2002.

Medearis, Angela. *Princess of the Press: The Story of Ida B. Wells Barnett*. New York: Lodestar Books, 1997.

Medearis, Angela. *The Freedom Riddle*. New York: Lodestar Books, 1995.

Mettger, Zak. *Reconstruction*. New York: Lodestar Books, 1994.

Michaels, Barbara, and Betty White. *Apples on a Stick: The Folklore of Black Children*. New York: Coward-McCann, Inc., 1983.

Miles, Johnnie H., Juanita J. Davis, Sharon E. Ferguson-Roberts, and Rita G. Giles. *Almanac of African American Heritage*. Paramus, NJ: Prentice Hall Press, 2001.

Miller, Robert. *Reflections of a Black Cowboy: Mountain Men*. New Jersey: Silver Burdett Press, Inc., 1992.

Miller, Robert. *Reflections of a Black Cowboy: Pioneers*. New Jersey: Silver Burdett Press, Inc., 1991.

Morris, Aldon. *The Origins of the Civil Rights Movement*. New York: The Free Press, 1984.

Myers, Walter. *Amistad: A Long Road to Freedom*. New York: Dutton Children's Books, 1998.

Myers, Walter. *Now Is Your Time! The African-American Struggle for Freedom*. New York: Harper Collins Publishers, 1991.

Nash, Gary B. *Forging Freedom*. Cambridge, Massachusetts: Harvard University Press, 1988.

Nash, Gary B. *Red, White, and Black*. Englewood Cliffs, New Jersey: Prentice-Hall, Inc., 1974.

Odum, Howard, and Guy Johnson. *The Negro and His Songs*. Hatboro, PA: Folklore Associates, 1964.

Opie, Iona, and Peter Opie. *The Oxford Dictionary of Nursery Rhymes*. New York: Oxford University Press, 1966.

Parrish, Lydia. *Slave Songs of the Georgia Sea Islands*. Hatboro, PA: Folklore Associates, 1965.

Patrick, Diane. *Amazing African American History: A Book of Answers for Kids*. New York: John Wiley & Sons, Inc., 1998.

Ploski, Harry A. and James Williams. *The Negro Almanac*. New York: Gale Research Inc., 1989.

Quarles, Benjamin. *Black Abolitionists*. New York: Da Capo Press, Inc., 1969.

Quarles, Benjamin. *The Negro in the American Revolution*. New York: W. W. Norton & Company, 1961.

Quarles, Benjamin. *The Negro in the Civil War*. Boston: Little, Brown and Company, 1969.

Quarles, Benjamin. *The Negro in the Making of America*. New York: Collier Books, 1964.

Rey, H. A. *Know the Stars*. New York: Scholastic, 1962.

Ripley, C. Peter, Ed. et al. *The Black Abolitionist Papers*. Chapel Hill: The University of North Carolina Press, 1986.

Rochelle, Belinda. *Witnesses to Freedom: Young People Who Fought for Civil Rights*. New York: Lodestar Books, 1993.

Saillant, John. *Black Puritan, Black Republican*. New York: Oxford University Press, 2003.

Salzman, Jack. *The African-American Experience*. New York: Macmillan Library Reference USA, 1993.

Scarborough, Dorothy. *On the Trail of Negro Folk-Songs*. Hatboro, PA: Folklore Associates, 1963.

Sertima, Ivan Van. *They Came Before Columbus*. New York: Random House, 1976.

Sherman, Joan R., Ed. *The Black Bard of North Carolina: George Moses Horton and His Poetry*. Chapel Hill, North Carolina: The University of North Carolina Press, 1997.

Smalls, Alexander. *Grace the Table*. New York: Harper Collins Publishers, 1997.

Smith, Jessie Carney. *Black Firsts*. Detroit: Visible Ink Press, 1994.

Smith, Jessie Carney. *Historical Statistics of Black America*. New York: Gale Research Inc., 1995.

Smith, Sande. *Who's Who in African American History*. New York: Smithmark, 1994.

Spalding, Henry D. *Encyclopedia of Black Folklore and Humor*. New York: Jonathan David Publishers, 1990.

Steward, Jeffrey. *1,001 Things Everyone Should Know About African American History*. New York: Doubleday, 1996.

Storrick, W. C. *Gettysburg: Battle and Battlefield*. New York: Barnes & Noble Books, 1994.

Taylor, Kimberly. *Black Abolitionists and Freedom Fighters*. Minneapolis, MN: The Oliver Press, Inc., 1996.

Terry, Rod. *Kwanzaa*. New York: Peter Pauper Press, Inc., 1996.

Thomas, Velma Maia. *Lest We Forget: The Passage from Africa to Slavery and Emancipation*. New York: Crown Publishers, Inc., 1997.

Time-Life Books. *African Americans: Voices of Triumph, Perseverance, Leadership, and Creative Fire*. Alexandria, VA: Time-Life Books, 1994.

Viola, Herman, and Carolyn Margolis. *Seeds of Change*. Washington, DC: Smithsonian Institution Press, 1991.

Weaver, Earl. *Jackie Robinson*. New York: Chelsea House Publishers, 1991.

Wesley, Charles H. and Patricia W. Romero. *International Library of Afro-American Life and History: Afro-Americans in the Civil War*. Cornwells Heights, PA: The Publishers Agency, Inc., 1978.

Wesley, Charles H. *International Library of Afro-American Life and History: In Freedom's Footsteps*. Cornwells Heights, PA: The Publishers Agency, Inc., 1978.

Wesley, Charles H. *International Library of Afro-American Life and History: The Quest for Equality*. Cornwells Heights, PA: The Publishers Agency, Inc., 1978.

Whitlow, Roger. *Black American Literature*. Chicago: Nelson Hall, 1973.

Williams, Michael W., Ed. *The African American Encyclopedia*. Volumes 1-8. New York: Marshall Cavendish, 1993.

Winch, Julie. *A Gentleman of Color: The Life of James Forten*. New York: Oxford University Press, 2002.

"Winfrey, Oprah." *Microsoft Encarta Encyclopedia 2000*. Microsoft Corporation, 1993–1999.

Wright, Kai. *Soldiers of Freedom*. New York: Black Dog and Leventhal Publishers, 2002.

Magazines

National Geographic, August 1990. "A Celebration of African-American Life." Roland L. Freeman, p. 66.

National Geographic, July 1984. "Escape from Slavery: Underground Railroad." Charles L. Blockson, p. 3.

National Geographic, August 1989. "I Dream a World." Brian Lanker, p. 209.

Internet

"African Americans, Festivals, and Parades in the North, 1741–1834." Shane, White. www.virginia.edu/~woodson/courses/aa405a/restricted/week+15/white.htm. (2 July 1998).

"African-AmericanHistory." www.sjr.com/news/99/02/14/d.htm. (24 November 1999).

"Africans in America/Part 1/Negroes at Jamestown Close-up." www.pbs.org/wgbh/aia/part1/1h289b.html. (11 March 2000).

"Africans in America/Part 2/Benjamin Banneker's Almanac Close-up." www.pbs.org/wgbh/aia/part2/2h68b.html. (2 October 1999).

"Africans in America/Part 2/Benjamin Banneker's Almanac." www.pbs.org/wgbh/aia/part2/2h68.html. (2 October 1999).

"AFRO-America: All Fun & Games." www.afroam.org/children/fun/kwanzaa/what.html. (1 January 2000).

"Anniversaries in African American History." www.saxakali.com/aaah.htm. (1 October 1999).

"Benjamin Banneker to the Secretary of State." www.lib.virginia.edu/etext/readex/24073.html. (15 February 1999).

"Benjamin Banneker." www.library.advanced.org/10320/Banneker.htm. (16 February 1999).

"Black History Tour." www.library.advanced.org/10320/Tour.htm. (15 February 1999).

"Black Inventors." www.swagga.com/inventors.htm. (8 December 1999).

"Black Voices—Kwanzaa." www.blackvoices.com/feature/kwanzaa/index.html. (1 January 2000).

"Breaking New Ground—African American Senators." www.senate.gov. (21 February 2007).

"Briana Scurry." www.womensoccer.com/biogs/scurry.html. (31 July 2006).

"BW32RO." www.pineridge7.com/newpage27.htm. (24 November 1999).

"Colin Powell—Washington Speakers Bureau, Inc." www.washspkrs.com/bio/c_pow.htm. (13 March 2000).

"Condoleezza Rice's Secret Weapon—Today's Christian." www.christianitytoday.com/tc/2002/005/1.18.html. (1 August 2006).

"Coretta Scott King Biography—Academy of Achievement." www.achievement.org/autodoc/page/kin1bio-1. (1 August 2006).

"Current Fellows: Darlene Clark Hine." wwwlradcliffe.edu/fellowships/current/bio.pha?id=59&year=2003-2004. (1 August 2006).

"Documenting the American South." http://docsouth.unc.edu/. (23 June 2006).

"Early Black Marshal." www.reporternews.com/texas/ law0302.html. (24 November 1999).

"ESPN.com-MLB-Barry Bonds-San Francisco Giants-Player Card." http://sports.espen.go.com/mlb/players/profile?statsld=3918. (29 July 2006).

"Explanation of 'Follow the Drinking Gourd.'" Quest.arc.nasa.gov/ltc/special/mlk/gourd2.html. (27 October 1999).

"First Black Americans." www.usnews.com. (21 February 2007).

"Follow the Drinking Gourd." www.contemplator.com/tunebook/ amermidi/gourd.htm. (27 October 1999).

"Follow the Drinking Gourd Song." Angelfire.com/pa/guavaberrybooks/gourd.html. (27 October 1999).

"Fort Mose." www.pbs.org/wgbh/aia/part2/2h14.html. (23 June 2006).

"Fort Mose Free African Settlement." www.oldcity.com/sites/ mose/. (23 June 2006).

"Henry Ford Museum & Greenfield Village." www.hfmgv.org/gifts/toys/hoop.html. (19 October 1999).

"Jessie Carney Smith." www.msu.edu/unit/msuaa/magazine/f92/jessie.htm. (1 August 2006).

"John and Mary Jones: Early Civil Rights Activists." www.encyclopedia.chicagohistory.org/pages/2458.html. (17 July 2006).

"Kwanzaa." www.whyy.org/smc/allen/ZwanWeb/kwanzaa.html#tambiko. (1 January 2000).

"Library of Congress Appoints Rita Dove Poet Laureate." www.loc.gov/today/pr/1993/93-071.html. (1 August 2006).

"Marble History!" www.iserv.net/~central/GAMES/marbles/marbhist.html. (2 October 1999).

"Merchant Mariners in the Revolutionary War."www.usmm.org/revolution.html. (1 October 1999).

"Most Worshipful Prince Hall Grand Lodge of PA." www.princehall-pa.org/GrandLodge/glhist.htm. (3 August 2006).

"Mystery of Va.'s First Slaves Is Unlocked 400 Years Later." www.washingtonpost.com. (21 February 2007).

"Online NewsHour: A Conversation with Ruby Bridges Hall—February 18, 1997." www.pbs.org/newshour/bb/race_relations/jan-june97/bridges_2-18.html. (13 March 2000).

"Oprah.com." www.oprah.com/about/ostory/about_ostory_herjourney.html. (13 March 2000).

"Outspoken: The Exhibit: Primary Sources." www.newberry.org/outspoken/exhibit/objectlist_section1.html. (13 March 2006).

"Player Bio: Tony Gwynn: Baseball." http://goaztexs.cstv.com/sports/m-basebl/mtt/gwynn_ tony00.html. (29 July 2006).

"Presidential Lectures: Henry Louis Gates, Jr.: Introduction." http://prelectur.stanford.edu/lecturers/gates/. (1 August 2006).

"Presidential Medal of Freedom Recipient Rosa Parks." www.medaloffreedom.com/RosaParks.htm. (1 August 2006).

"Roberto Clemente." http://library.thinkquest.org/2667/ Clemente.htm. (29 July 2006).

"Rosa Parks Biography." www.achievement.org/autodoc/ page/par0bio-1. (14 December 1999).

"Salem Poor: 'A Brave and Gallant Soldier.'" www.nps.gov/ revwar/images/about_the_rev/salem_poor.gif. (14 June 2006).

"Secretary of State Condoleezza Rice." www.state.gov/r/pa/ei/ biog/41252.htm. (1 August 2006).

"Settlement of Virginia." Jefferson.village.virginia.edu/vcdh/ jamestown/images3/AtlasofVA/AtlasofVAp_20bg.jpg. (11 March 2000).

"Seventeen from Negro Leagues, Pre-Negro Leagues Eras Elected to the Hall of Fame by Special Committee." www.baseballhalloffame.org/news/2006/060227.htm. (29 July 2006).

"Shaquille O'Neal-Miami Heat-NBA-Yahoo! Sports." http://sports.yahoo.com/nab/players/847. (29 July 2006.)

"Stamp on Black History: The History of African American Cooking." Library.advanced.org/10320/History.htm. (18 October 1999).

"The American Variety Stage: Vaudeville and Popular Entertainment, 1870–1920." lcweb2.loc.gov/cgi-bin/ query/D?varstg:1:./temp/~ammem_taDL. (19 October 1999).

"The Black Heritage Trail: George Middleton House." www.nps.gov/boaf/site2.htm. (12 May 2006).

"The History Makers." www.thehistorymakers.com/biography/giobraphy.asp?bioindex=196. (3 August 2006).

"The Jamestown Experience." Jefferson.village.virginia.edu/vcdh/jamestown/maps/jsmap1.html. (11 March 2000).

"The Marshals Monitor." www.financenet.gov/exsales/www.usdoj.gov/article1.html. (24 November 1999).

"The Meaning of Kwanzaa." www.si.edu/anacostia/kwanz.htm. (21 July 1999).

"The Women of the Hall—Rosa Parks." www.greatwomen.org/parks.htm. (14 December 1999).

"Wentworth Cheswell-Cheswell Family Cemetery, Newmarket New Hampshire." www.gravematter.com/cheswell.htm. (24 June 2006).

"Where is Jamestown?" www.apva.org/tour/whereis.html. (11 March 2000).

❖ Index ❖